2-3 INSTANT Math Centers

HANDS-ON INDEPENDENT MATH ACTIVITIES

CONTRIBUTING WRITERS

Janet Bruno, Laura Means, Liz Newman, and Glenda Nugent

EDITOR
Ruth Simon

ILLUSTRATOR
Kathleen Dunne

COVER ILLUSTRATOR
Eddie Young

DESIGNER
Marek/Janci Design

COVER DESIGNER
Moonhee Pak

ART DIRECTOR
Tom Cochrane

PROJECT DIRECTOR
Carolea Williams

CTP © 2000 Creative Teaching Press, Inc., Huntington Beach, CA 92649

Reproduction of activities in any manner for use in the classroom and not for commercial sale is permissible.

Reproduction of these materials for an entire school or for a school system is strictly prohibited.

Table of Contents

Introduction 3
How Do I Begin? • How Do I Implement the Center Activities? • How Do I Keep Track?

Addition 10
Shake and Spill • Domino Addition • Bundle Addition • Place Value Addition

Calculators 19
Tic-Tac-Toe • Sum Target • Calculator Race • Grocery Shopping

Division 29
Sharing Cookies • Equal Teams • Division with Remainders

Estimating 36
Estimation Jars • Estimating Area • Estimating Time

Fractions 43
Pattern Block Fractions • Window Fractions • Sharing Pizza

Geometry 50
Hexagon Cover-Up • Symmetrical Designs • Congruent Shapes

Graphing 56
Bean Graph • Color Cube Graph • Student Survey • Graphing Bags

Logic 65
Fill It In • Toothpick Puzzlers • Show the Ways

Measurement 72
Different Shapes—Different Levels • Which Is More? • How Many Cubes? •
Weighing a Pound • Lightest to Heaviest

Money 82
How Many Ways? • Pay in Two Ways • Toy Store

Multiplication 89
Equal Groups • Multiplication Designs • Multiplication Arrays • Under the Sea Multiplication

Place Value 99
Building Numbers • Place Value Pictures • High Card

Probability 106
Guess the Colors • Three-Color Cube • Heads or Tails

Subtraction 113
Subtraction Sock • Dice Subtraction • Subtraction Designs • A Dollar to Spend

Time 122
Showing Time • 30 Minutes Later • Keeping Track of Your Day

Introduction

Instant Math Centers is designed to offer a great supplement to your primary math program, providing reinforcement of basic math skills through practical, hands-on application in a format students will enjoy.

Instant Math Centers consists of 52 center activities within 15 math skill areas. Each skill section begins with a one-page overview of the center activities in that math skill area, including materials needed and teaching tips and extensions. The ☆ icon indicates teacher preparation that is required for an activity. The bulleted items are optional teaching tips and extensions. Each center activity includes a task card and accompanying activity sheets—all reproducible for instant student use.

 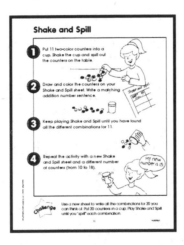 

Each task card presents step-by-step directions, simply written and clearly illustrated, plus a Challenge or Math Journal activity. The illustrations show students exactly what to do, making the activities easy to follow, even for beginning readers and those with limited English language skills.

Instant Math Centers is designed to help students build a strong mathematical foundation and gives them experiences in all content and process areas of the National Council of Teachers of Mathematics standards as follows:

- number and operation
- patterns, functions, and algebra
- geometry and spatial sense
- measurement
- data analysis, statistics, and probability

- problem solving
- reasoning and proof
- communication
- connections
- representations

How Do I Begin?

Create a Math Center

A classroom math center should include a variety of materials for students to manipulate and enough space in which to work. There should be opportunities for free exploration and discovery, as well as specifically directed activities, which is where *Instant Math Centers* offers the perfect solution.

The physical setup could be as limited, small, and isolated as a desk with a study carrel around it, one or more math center activities, and the materials for those activities.

If space allows, you can use an entire corner of the classroom for your math center. A center with tables, countertop space, and a carpeted area allows students to work on a variety of activities. Store activity materials on shelves and in drawers and containers for easy access by students.

Gather Materials

The initial preparation is simply to reproduce the pages needed for the activities you have chosen. Feel free to enhance the task cards and activity sheets by coloring them. For durability and long-term use, mount them on tagboard, and then laminate them or store them in plastic or acetate pocket sheet protectors.

In addition to a generous supply of paper and pencils, the materials needed to implement *Instant Math Centers* in your classroom are a combination of common household items and commercial math manipulatives, such as linking cubes and pattern blocks. The easiest way to begin is to send home a letter with a list of requested items at the beginning of the year. Use the reproducible letter to parents on page 5, or create one of your own. Prepare a sorting area, and have students help you organize the materials.

Dear Parents,

We are asking for your help in collecting materials to use in our math program. We will use these materials for adding, subtracting, sorting, measuring, estimating, and counting. Please don't purchase items especially for us. Just see if you have any of these items at home that you may no longer need. If you can, please send any of the items listed below.

- buttons, beads, spools, clothespins, marbles, shells, yarn, string, shoelaces, socks

- small rocks, stones, pinecones, nuts, bolts, screws, washers, old keys, bottle caps, small lids, poker chips, dice

- pasta (macaroni in assorted colors and shapes, shells, spirals, etc.), dry beans in assorted colors (pinto, navy, black, red, lima, etc.), popcorn (unpopped), seeds, rice, mixed nuts (shelled and unshelled), trail mix, snack mix

- measuring cups, measuring spoons, scoops, funnels, straws, coffee stirrers, craft sticks, toothpicks (flat)

- various coins, play money

- plastic containers—cups, bowls, and empty margarine tubs, food containers with lids, and film canisters

- small plastic or cardboard boxes (shoe-box size or smaller) for storing items

- paper cups, paper plates, paper bags (lunch size), resealable plastic bags

Thank you for your help.

Sincerely,

Instant Math Centers • 2–3 © 2000 Creative Teaching Press

How Do I Implement the Center Activities?

The simplest way to introduce your students to the activities in *Instant Math Centers* is in small groups on a rotating basis. Select activities that are appropriate for the skill level of each group. During these initial experiences, set guidelines for how to use the center, how to care for materials, and where to put finished products. Once students are familiar with the procedures, experiment with teacher-directed and self-directed options, student groupings, the number of activities, and time and space allowances.

How many students work in the math center at a time depends largely on the amount of space and materials in the center. You can limit the number of students by the number of chairs available, or make a designated number of math center necklaces or color-coded clothespins available for them to wear during their time in the math center. Students can work individually, in pairs (with a classmate or a cross-age tutor), or in small groups. You will be able to observe each student's degree of independent functioning and use this data to determine future groupings. Students who excel in a particular activity may be paired with those being introduced to that activity for the first time or with those who may need additional direction for completing the task. If space and supplies are ample and students are productively engaged, everyone wins.

The number of center activities available to the students can vary from one to many, at any given time, depending on the degree of simultaneous activity that you are comfortable with. Regardless of how many center activities are available to students, they should all be meaningful and appropriate and should reinforce or provide practice in skill areas that have already been presented.

The length of time you allot for math center activities may vary, depending on the students and the tasks. You can learn a lot about your students and their learning styles, their degree of responsibility, and their thought processes by allowing them some freedom to choose activities and then observing them as they work.

The purpose for having centers in the classroom is to provide a meaningful setting in which students can apply skills that they have already been taught. While students are thus engaged, the teacher is free to work with small groups of students, as well as circulate throughout the classroom to observe, record anecdotal notes, and offer direction as needed.

Ideally, students will have the freedom to explore a variety of hands-on activities and make choices about which activities they pursue. Making choices is as important a skill as any math skill. It is an essential part of learning to think and take responsibility for oneself.

How Do I Keep Track?

Many effective means of assessment are available to you. How you choose to keep track will depend on what information you value as most important to record. The reproducible activity sheets in *Instant Math Centers* can be stored in individual student folders or in a central location in the math center. These pages provide a built-in record of students' accomplishments and levels of understanding.

Teacher observation and anecdotal records can serve as invaluable tools with which to assess the needs of students, as well as a means to gain insights into their unique learning styles and thought processes. Note what choices students make. Some students may systematically go through the center activities sequentially. Some may select activities at random. Others may choose the same activity over and over again. As students are engaged in a center activity, encourage them to verbalize their findings by asking them appropriate questions about how they arrived at their conclusions.

Use the Student Checklist on page 9 to keep track of completed activities. It may be used to simply indicate which math center activities each student chooses and how often. You can also use a coding system, such as –, ?, +, or 0, /, X, to denote level of mastery, or devise your own system.

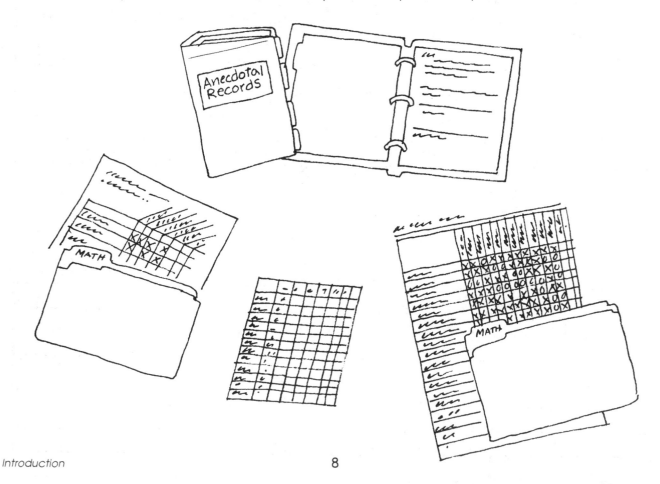

Student Checklist

Instant Math Centers • 2–3 © 2000 Creative Teaching Press

Addition

These center activities offer students a variety of concrete experiences creating, solving, and writing addition problems. They provide practice in addition of two-digit numbers, with and without regrouping. The use of manipulatives will help students learn the sequence of steps and visualize the reasons for the steps in addition of two-digit numbers. Students need a good understanding of place value in order to be successful with the concept of regrouping.

Shake and Spill
Teaching Tips and Extensions

- To make inexpensive two-color counters, spray-paint large lima beans on one side only.
- Have students repeat the activity several times, concentrating on one fact family at a time (e.g., all the facts for 15).

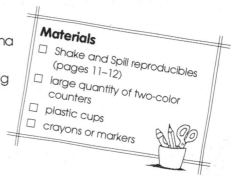

Materials
- ☐ Shake and Spill reproducibles (pages 11–12)
- ☐ large quantity of two-color counters
- ☐ plastic cups
- ☐ crayons or markers

Domino Addition
Teaching Tips and Extensions

- Make paper dominoes if real ones are not available. Draw dots with a white crayon or paint on black construction paper rectangles.
- Invite each student to place circle stickers on an index card to make an additional "domino" for the math center.

Materials
- ☐ Domino Addition reproducibles (pages 13–14)
- ☐ set of dominoes
- ☐ resealable plastic bag
- ☐ beans

Bundle Addition
Teaching Tips and Extensions

- Have students take three or four handfuls of straws to practice adding larger numbers.

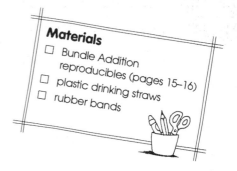

Materials
- ☐ Bundle Addition reproducibles (pages 15–16)
- ☐ plastic drinking straws
- ☐ rubber bands

Place Value Addition
Teaching Tips and Extensions

- ☆ Place two sets of number cards in each envelope. Make sure the cards fit in the boxes on the Addition Frame reproducible.
- Laminate copies of the Addition Frame reproducible.
- Ask students to tell you their strategy for making the highest total possible with any four cards.

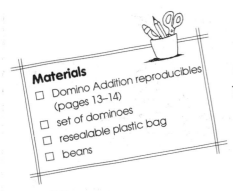

Materials
- ☐ Place Value Addition reproducibles (pages 17–18)
- ☐ several teacher-made number cards, 0–9
- ☐ envelopes
- ☐ calculators and/or place value cubes

Shake and Spill

1 Put 11 two-color counters into a cup. Shake the cup and spill out the counters on the table.

2 Draw and color the counters on your Shake and Spill sheet. Write a matching addition number sentence.

3 Keep playing Shake and Spill until you have found all the different combinations for 11.

4 Repeat the activity with a new Shake and Spill sheet and a different number of counters (from 10 to 18).

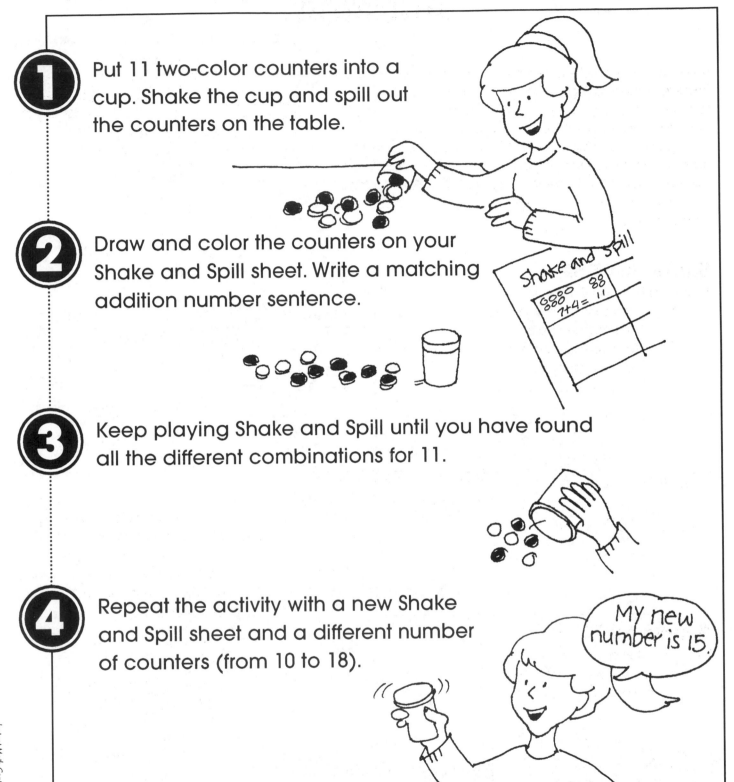

Challenge Use a new sheet to write all the combinations for 20 you can think of. Put 20 counters in a cup. Play Shake and Spill until you "spill" each combination.

Instant Math Centers • 2–3 © 2000 Creative Teaching Press

Addition

Shake and Spill

Instant Math Centers • 2–3 © 2000 Creative Teaching Press

Domino Addition

1 Take 2 dominoes from the bag.

2 Place beans on your Domino Addition sheet to match the dots on the dominoes you selected.

3 Add up the total number of beans. Write a number sentence for your addition problem.

4 Repeat the activity 9 more times.

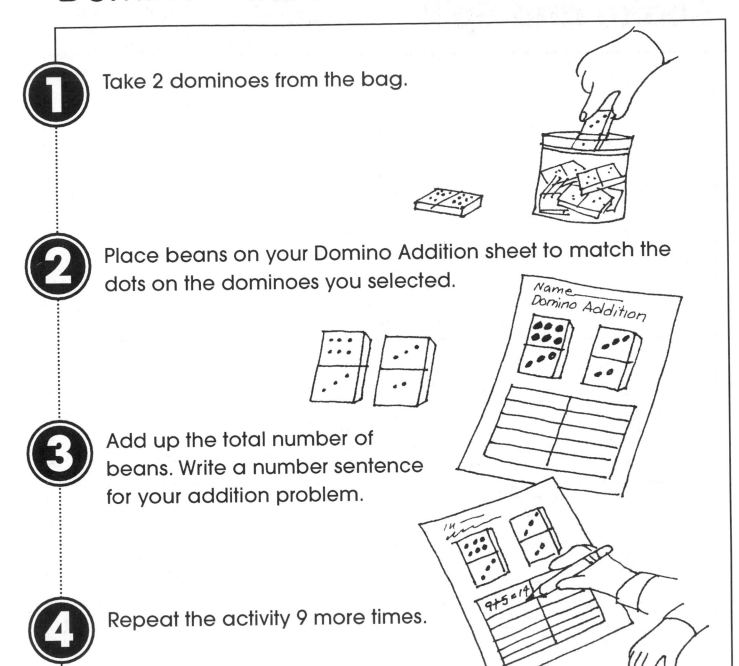

Instant Math Centers • 2–3 © 2000 Creative Teaching Press

Challenge Take 3 dominoes from the bag and add the number of dots. Add the dots on 4, 5, or 6 dominoes.

Addition

Domino Addition

Instant Math Centers • 2–3 © 2000 Creative Teaching Press

Bundle Addition

1 Take a handful of straws and bundle them into groups of 10 with the rubber bands. The leftover straws will be 1s.

2 Repeat step 1 and write the 2 numbers as an addition problem on a piece of paper.

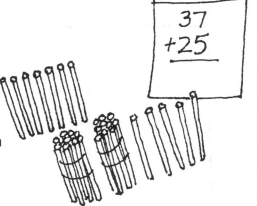

$$\begin{array}{r} 37 \\ +25 \\ \hline \end{array}$$

3 Add all the straws together, making more bundles of 10 if you can. Write the answer.

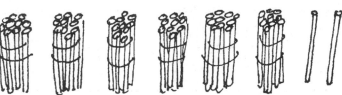

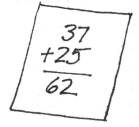

$$\begin{array}{r} 37 \\ +25 \\ \hline 62 \end{array}$$

4 Repeat the activity 8 or 10 times.

Math Journal Explain on your journal page why it is helpful to regroup the straws into 10s and 1s.

Instant Math Centers • 2–3 © 2000 Creative Teaching Press

Addition

Math Journal

Explain why it is helpful to regroup the straws into tens and ones.

_____

_____

_____

_____

_____

_____

_____

_____

_____

_____

_____

_____

_____

_____

_____

_____

Instant Math Centers • 2–3 © 2000 Creative Teaching Press

Place Value Addition

1 Mix up all the number cards in 1 envelope. Place them in a pile facedown.

2 Pick 4 cards and place them faceup on your Addition Frame sheet.

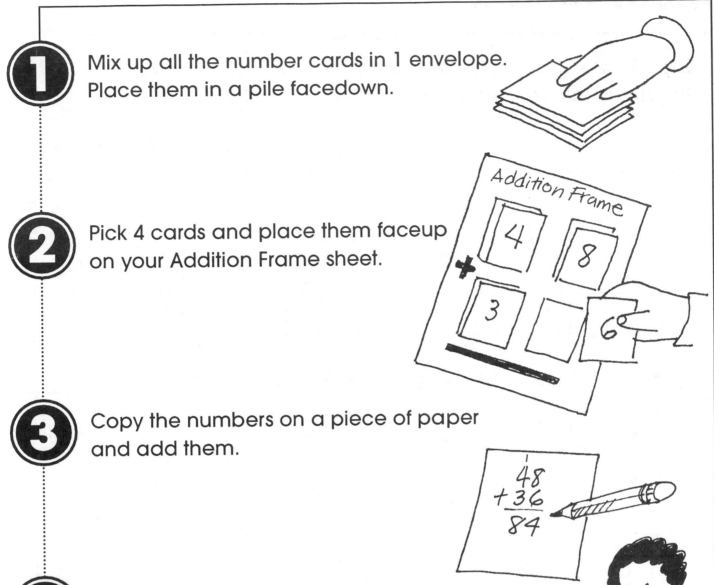

3 Copy the numbers on a piece of paper and add them.

4 Use a calculator or place value cubes to check your answer. Repeat the activity at least 5 more times.

Challenge Play a game with a partner. Pick 4 cards each and place them on your sheet to get the highest addition total. Continue playing, trying to make the highest total each time.

Addition

Instant Math Centers • 2–3 © 2000 Creative Teaching Press

Addition Frame

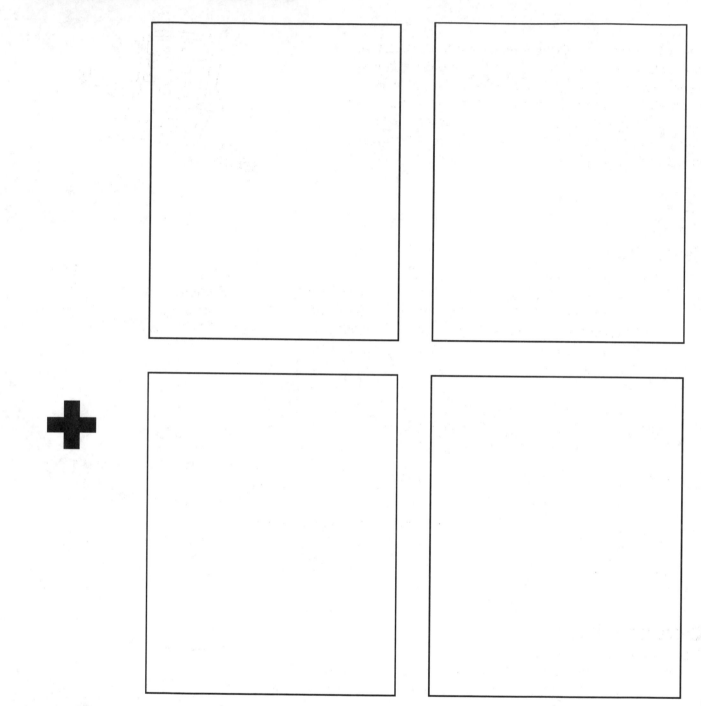

Instant Math Centers • 2–3 © 2000 Creative Teaching Press

Calculators

Calculators are basic tools in today's society. When young students use calculators for computation in these center activities, it is important to stress estimation skills and the identification of reasonable answers. In problem-solving activities, the use of calculators allows students to focus on important mathematical ideas rather than on tedious calculations.

Tic-Tac-Toe
Teaching Tips and Extensions
☆ Use the Tic-Tac-Toe reproducible in two ways: make blank copies of it as it is, and make copies of it after you fill it in with problems appropriate for your students. Use addition, subtraction, multiplication, and/or division problems, or a combination.

● Encourage students to fill in their own problems on blank copies of the Tic-Tac-Toe reproducible to create new tic-tac-toe games.

Materials
- ☐ Tic-Tac-Toe reproducibles (pages 20–21)
- ☐ calculators

Sum Target
Teaching Tips and Extensions
☆ Make a set of 8–10 number cards for each pair of students. Pick sums that are appropriate for your students. (For example, second graders might concentrate on sums to 20, and third graders could work with higher numbers.)

● Extend the activity by asking students to use multiplication to find the target number.

Materials
- ☐ Sum Target reproducibles (pages 22–23)
- ☐ teacher-made number cards, bagged in sets
- ☐ small paper bags
- ☐ calculators

Calculator Race
Teaching Tips and Extensions
● Have students play a different version of the game. Make the first player to reach 0 be the loser. Ask students to explain any change in strategy.

Materials
- ☐ Calculator Race reproducibles (pages 24–25)
- ☐ calculators

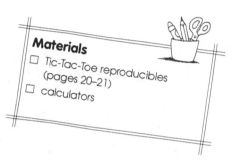

Grocery Shopping
Teaching Tips and Extensions
● Use an assortment of current grocery store ads instead of the Grocery Shopping reproducible on page 27.

● Show students how to calculate the prices of items sold by the pound.

Materials
- ☐ Grocery Shopping reproducibles (pages 26–28)
- ☐ calculators

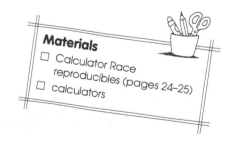

Tic-Tac-Toe

1 Play with a partner. Player X solves a problem on the Tic-Tac-Toe sheet without using a calculator.

2 Both players: Check the problem with a calculator. If the answer is correct, make an X in the square. If the answer is incorrect, make an O in the square.

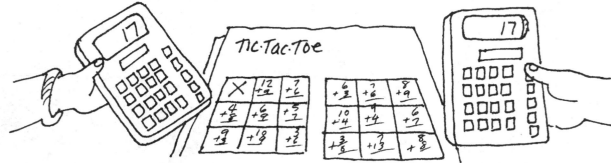

3 Player O takes a turn. Keep taking turns until one player has 3 in a row. Pick a different sheet and play again.

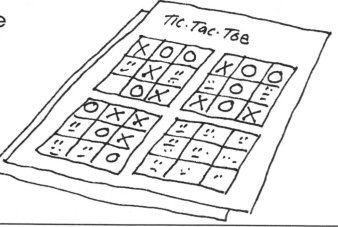

Fill in a blank sheet with your own problems, and play with a partner.

Instant Math Centers • 2–3 © 2000 Creative Teaching Press

Player X _____ Player O _____

Tic-Tac-Toe

Game 1

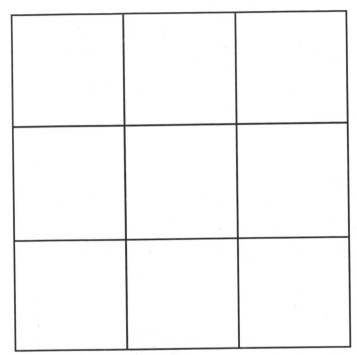

Game 2

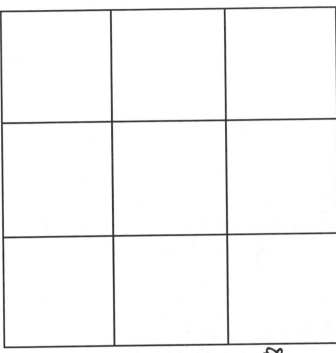

Game 3

Game 4

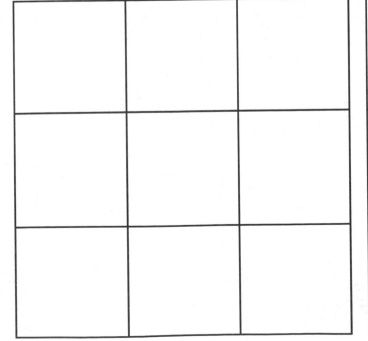

Instant Math Centers • 2-3 © 2000 Creative Teaching Press

Calculators

Sum Target

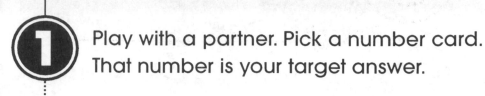

1 Play with a partner. Pick a number card. That number is your target answer.

2 Enter on a calculator any number that is less than your target answer. Then press $+$.

3 See if your partner can reach the target answer by entering a number and pressing $=$. If successful, your partner writes the addition sentence on a Sum Target sheet.

4 Trade places and keep taking turns playing Sum Target.

Challenge Enter any number below 100. See if your partner can enter a number that will add up to exactly 100. Keep taking turns.

Instant Math Centers • 2–3 © 2000 Creative Teaching Press

Sum Target

Player A _____   Player B _____

_____   _____

_____   _____

_____   _____

_____   _____

_____   _____

_____   _____

_____   _____

_____   _____

_____   _____

_____   _____

Instant Math Centers • 2–3 © 2000 Creative Teaching Press

Calculators

Calculator Race

1 Work with a partner. Enter 50 on a calculator.

2 Take turns subtracting any 1-digit number except 0. The player who reaches 0 first is the winner.

50 - 6 =

3 Play Calculator Race 5 more times. Take turns going first.

This time I'll be first.

4 Play again 3 more times. Start with a different number each time.

Math Journal Describe your strategy for playing Calculator Race on your journal page.

Instant Math Centers • 2–3 © 2000 Creative Teaching Press

Name _____

Math Journal

Describe your strategy for playing Calculator Race.

_____

_____

_____

_____

_____

_____

_____

_____

_____

_____

_____

_____

_____

_____

Instant Math Centers • 2–3 © 2000 Creative Teaching Press

Calculators

Grocery Shopping

1 Look at the grocery ads. Make a list of 10 items you plan to buy on your Shopping List sheet.

2 Write the price of each item on your list.

3 Calculate the total price of the groceries.

4 Calculate the change if you pay with a $20.00 bill (or two $20.00 bills).

Challenge

Work with a partner. See who can buy the most groceries for $50.00.

Instant Math Centers • 2–3 © 2000 Creative Teaching Press

Grocery Shopping

Orange Juice $1.29

Lemonade 59¢

Yogurt 59¢

Apples 69¢/LB.
Grapes 89¢/LB.
Bananas 39¢/LB.

Cookies $2.79

Tortilla Chips $1.79

Crackers $2.34

Oat Cereal $1.99

Pudding.......89¢
Popcorn....$1.19
Soup.....$1.19
Macaroni and Cheese....79¢
Chili.....$1.59
Spaghetti....99¢

Ice Cream $3.99

Milk $1.99

Chicken 99¢/LB

Instant Math Centers • 2-3 © 2000 Creative Teaching Press

Name _____

Shopping List

Price

1. _____   _____

2. _____   _____

3. _____   _____

4. _____   _____

5. _____   _____

6. _____   _____

7. _____   _____

8. _____   _____

9. _____   _____

10. _____   _____

                                     Total _____

Instant Math Centers • 2–3 © 2000 Creative Teaching Press

Division

These center activities include both kinds of division problems: sharing and grouping (e.g., you can share 12 pencils among 4 students or divide a class of 24 students into groups of 6). Students should be introduced to both types of division. The concept of remainders should also be a natural part of first experiences with division.

Sharing Cookies
Teaching Tips and Extensions
- As a special treat, use real mini-cookies or cookie cereal.
- Have students record the division problems.
- Introduce the activity by reading aloud *The Doorbell Rang* by Pat Hutchins.

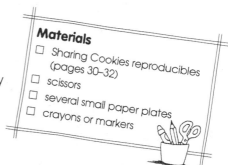

Materials
- ☐ Sharing Cookies reproducibles (pages 30–32)
- ☐ scissors
- ☐ several small paper plates
- ☐ crayons or markers

Materials
- ☐ Equal Teams reproducibles (pages 33–34)
- ☐ scissors

Equal Teams
Teaching Tips and Extensions
- Show students both ways to record division problems: sharing and grouping.
- Use sets of 24 counters in place of the Equal Teams reproducible on page 34.

Division with Remainders
Teaching Tips and Extensions
- If you do not have colored tiles, cut colored construction paper into 1" (2.5 cm) squares.
- Show students how to record division problems with remainders.
- As students gain experience, have them start the activity with a greater number of colored tiles.

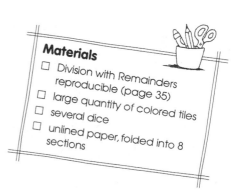

Materials
- ☐ Division with Remainders reproducible (page 35)
- ☐ large quantity of colored tiles
- ☐ several dice
- ☐ unlined paper, folded into 8 sections

Sharing Cookies

1 Cut out the cookies.

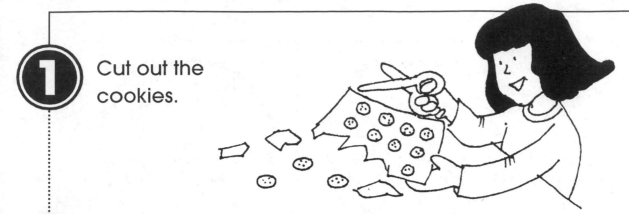

2 How would 2 friends share the cookies? Place the cookies on paper plates to show your answer.

3 Draw the cookies on your Sharing Cookies sheet.

Name   Tricia
Sharing Cookies

4 Repeat the activity. Show how to share the cookies with 3 friends, 4 friends, and 6 friends.

Challenge   Show how you would share the cookies among 5 people. Draw your answer on the back of your sheet.

Instant Math Centers • 2–3 © 2000 Creative Teaching Press

Cookies

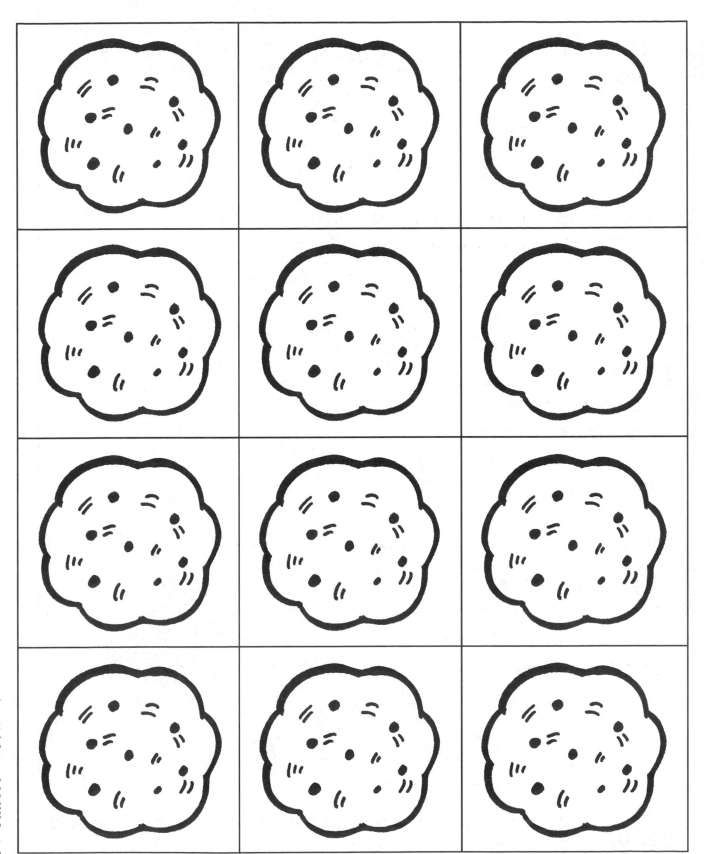

Instant Math Centers • 2–3 © 2000 Creative Teaching Press

Division

Name _____

Sharing Cookies

2 Friends

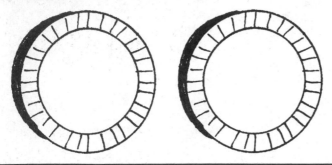

3 Friends

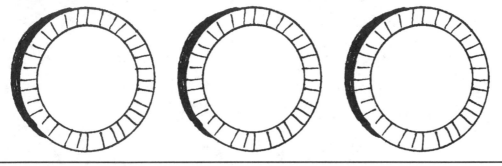

4 Friends

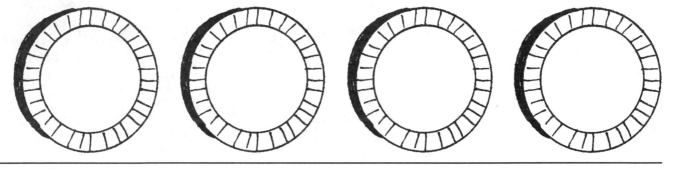

6 Friends

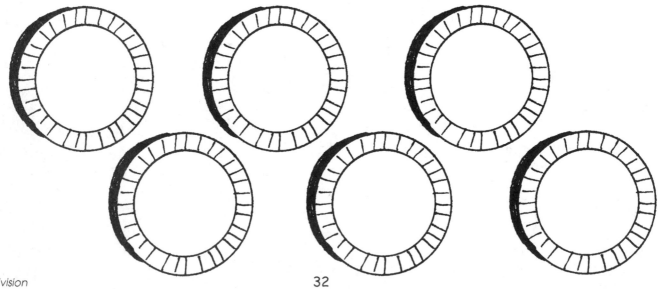

Instant Math Centers • 2–3 © 2000 Creative Teaching Press

Equal Teams

1 Cut out the pictures of the 24 team players.

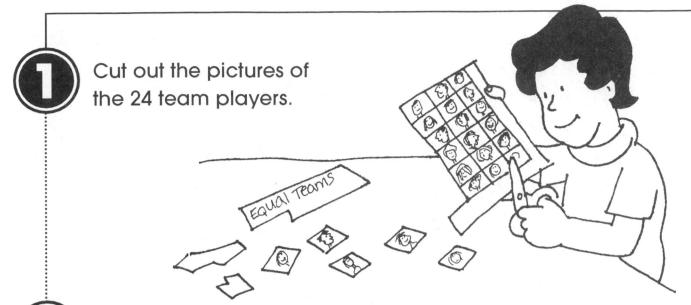

2 Divide the group of players so that there are 12 on a team. How many teams will there be? Write the division problem on a piece of paper.

3 Repeat the activity with 8 on a team, 6 on a team, and 4 on a team. Write the division problem each time.

Challenge

Work with a partner. Describe a fair way to divide your class into equal teams. Write the names of the students on the teams on a sheet of paper. Repeat the activity and divide your class into a different number of teams.

Instant! Math Centers • 2–3 © 2000 Creative Teaching Press

Division

Equal Teams

Instant Math Centers • 2–3 © 2000 Creative Teaching Press

Division with Remainders

1 Start with 15 colored tiles. Roll a die and arrange the tiles into that many equal rows. Show the remainder, if there is one.

2 Draw the array and write the division problem on a piece of paper. Do not forget to show the remainder, if there is one.

Dawn

$15 \div 2 = 7 R1$

$2\overline{)15}\ \ 7 R1$

3 Pick a new number of tiles, and repeat the activity 7 more times.

Challenge   Use the tiles to show 3 division problems that have a remainder of 1. Draw the arrays and write the division problems on a piece of paper.

Division

Estimating

One of the most important concepts that students learn through estimation activities is that it is not always necessary to find an exact answer. Help students develop basic strategies for arriving at reasonable estimates and refining their estimates. These center activities focus on estimating quantity, area, and duration of time.

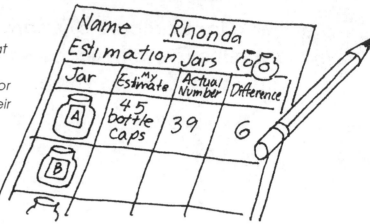

Estimation Jars
Teaching Tips and Extensions

☆ Fill each jar with a different kind of object. Use a total number of objects appropriate for your students.

- As an alternative, vary the sizes of the jars but use the same objects in all the jars.
- Have an estimation contest with a jar of jelly beans or other treat.

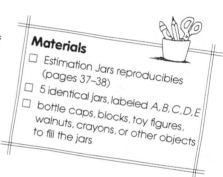

Materials
- ☐ Estimation Jars reproducibles (pages 37–38)
- ☐ 5 identical jars, labeled A, B, C, D, E
- ☐ bottle caps, blocks, toy figures, walnuts, crayons, or other objects to fill the jars

Estimating Area
Teaching Tips and Extensions

- Make sure students securely tape the ends of each piece of yarn together.
- Have students work on a textured surface. The yarn shape tends to change on smooth surfaces.
- Ask students to describe the difference between the shape that held the most cubes and the shape that held the least cubes.

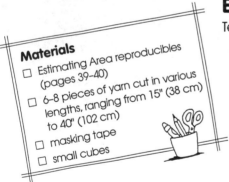

Materials
- ☐ Estimating Area reproducibles (pages 39–40)
- ☐ 6–8 pieces of yarn cut in various lengths, ranging from 15" (38 cm) to 40" (102 cm)
- ☐ masking tape
- ☐ small cubes

Estimating Time
Teaching Tips and Extensions

- Teach students how to operate a stopwatch. If the wall clock has a second hand, students could use it to time the activities.
- Remind students to use the most appropriate unit of time (seconds or minutes) when making estimates.

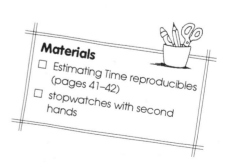

Materials
- ☐ Estimating Time reproducibles (pages 41–42)
- ☐ stopwatches with second hands

Estimation Jars

1 Pick a jar. Estimate how many objects are in the jar. Write your estimate on your Estimation Jars sheet.

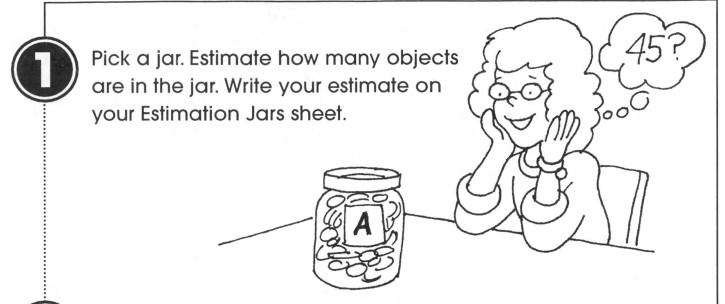

2 Count the objects in the jar and write the actual number. Compare your estimate with the actual number. Write the difference between the two numbers.

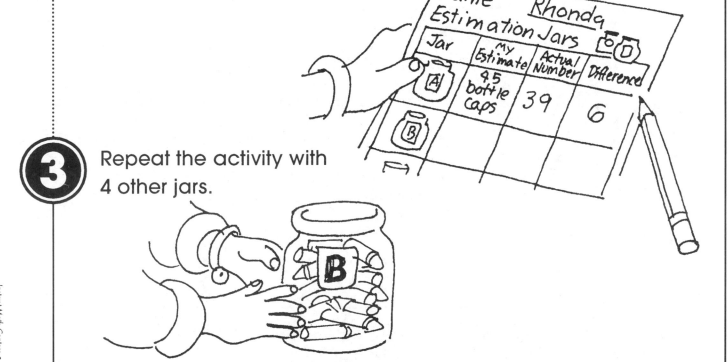

Name	Rhonda		
Estimation Jars			
Jar	My Estimate	Actual Number	Difference
A	45 bottle caps	39	6
B			

3 Repeat the activity with 4 other jars.

Instant Math Centers • 2–3 © 2000 Creative Teaching Press

Challenge Work with a partner. Each of you fill a jar with objects. Estimate how many objects are in each other's jar. Count the objects and see who comes closest to the actual number.

Estimating

Estimation Jars

Jar	My Estimate	Actual Number	Difference
A			
B			
C			
D			
E			

Instant Math Centers • 2–3 © 2000 Creative Teaching Press

Estimating Area

1 Pick a piece of yarn and tape the ends together to make a closed shape. Estimate how many cubes will fill your shape.

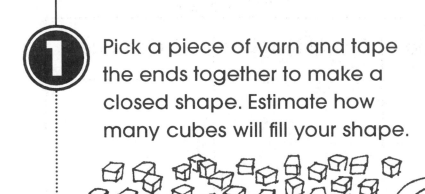

2 Draw your shape and write your estimate on your Estimating Area sheet.

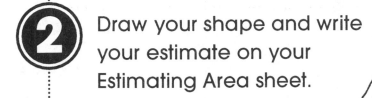

3 Fill the shape with 1 layer of cubes. Count the total number of cubes and write the number on your sheet.

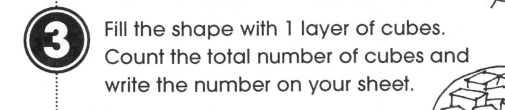

4 Use the same piece of yarn to repeat the activity 2 more times. Make a different shape each time.

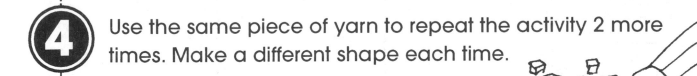

Challenge Work with a partner. Take 2 strings of different lengths. Can you make 2 different shapes that will hold the same number of cubes?

Estimating

Instant Math Centers • 2–3 © 2000 Creative Teaching Press

Name _____

Estimating Area

My Shape	My Estimate	Actual Number

Instant Math Centers • 2–3 © 2000 Creative Teaching Press

Estimating Time

 1 Work with a partner. Select an activity from the Estimating Time sheet. Estimate how long it will take (in seconds or minutes) to complete the activity. Write your estimate on your sheet.

 2 Have your partner time how long it takes you to complete the activity. Write the actual time.

 3 Take turns repeating steps 1 and 2. Each partner does 4 activities.

 **Challenge** With a partner, think of an activity that takes about 15 seconds to complete. Time each other to be sure. Then think of a 30-second or a 1-minute activity.

Instant Math Centers • 2–3 © 2000 Creative Teaching Press

Estimating

Names_____ _____

Estimating Time

Activity	My Estimate	Actual Time
Tie your shoe.		
Write your whole name. Ann Marie Adams		
Sing "Happy Birthday."		
Count backwards from 50 to 0. 50, 49, 48..		
Touch your toes 20 times.		
Do 10 sit-ups.		
Write the alphabet. Q R S T U V W X Y Z		
Say the Pledge of Allegiance.		

Instant Math Centers • 2–3 © 2000 Creative Teaching Press

Fractions

These center activities focus on the identification of basic fractions as equal parts of a whole and equal parts of a set. As students explore the concept of fractions, it is important for them to be able to handle concrete materials so they can compare and identify fractional parts.

Pattern Block Fractions
Teaching Tips and Extensions

- If you don't have a class set of pattern blocks, use the reproducible pattern blocks. Trace or photocopy each shape on a different color of paper, and laminate the papers. Cut out a large supply of each shape, and place shapes in individual plastic bags.

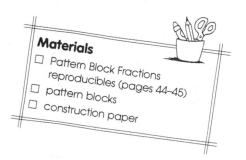

Materials
- ☐ Pattern Block Fractions reproducibles (pages 44–45)
- ☐ pattern blocks
- ☐ construction paper

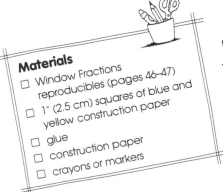

Materials
- ☐ Window Fractions reproducibles (pages 46–47)
- ☐ 1" (2.5 cm) squares of blue and yellow construction paper
- ☐ glue
- ☐ construction paper
- ☐ crayons or markers

Window Fractions
Teaching Tips and Extensions

- Introduce the activity by reading aloud *The Half Birthday Party* by Charlotte Pomerantz.

Sharing Pizza
Teaching Tips and Extensions

- Discuss what makes a "fair share."

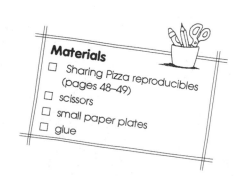

Materials
- ☐ Sharing Pizza reproducibles (pages 48–49)
- ☐ scissors
- ☐ small paper plates
- ☐ glue

Pattern Block Fractions

1 Use the pattern blocks to make as many shapes as you can that have 2 equal parts (halves).

2 Make as many shapes as you can that have 3 equal parts (thirds).

 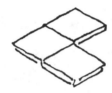 

3 Make as many shapes as you can that have 4 equal parts (fourths).

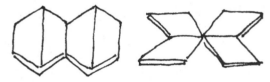

4 Make shapes to show these other fractions: fifths, eighths, and tenths. Show them to a classmate.

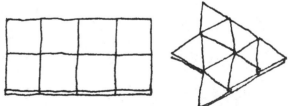

Challenge Trace around the pattern blocks from steps 1–4 on construction paper. Label each fractional part.

Instant Math Centers • 2–3 © 2000 Creative Teaching Press

Pattern Blocks

Instant Math Centers • 2–3 © 2000 Creative Teaching Press

Fractions

Window Fractions

1 Place blue and yellow squares in the windows on your Window Fractions Work Mat. Make sure each house looks different.

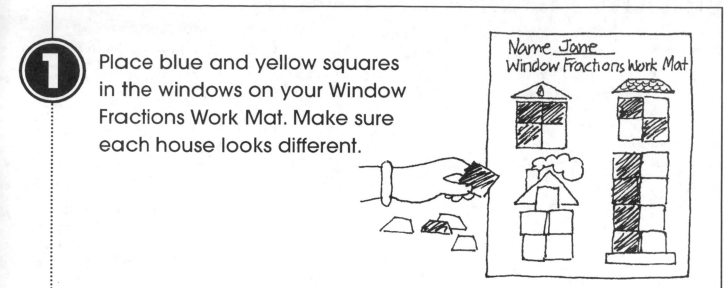

2 Glue the squares on your work mat.

3 Write fractions to show how many windows in each house are blue and how many are yellow.

 **Challenge** Draw a house with 10 windows on construction paper. Place the blue and yellow squares in the windows. List all possible fractions.

Instant Math Centers • 2–3 © 2000 Creative Teaching Press

Window Fractions Work Mat

_____ blue   _____ yellow

_____ blue   _____ yellow

_____ blue   _____ yellow

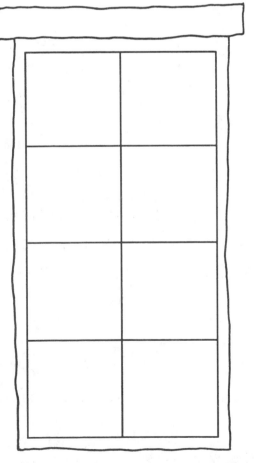

_____ blue   _____ yellow

Instant Math Centers • 2–3 © 2000 Creative Teaching Press

Fractions

Sharing Pizza

1 Cut out the 12 pieces of the pizza.

2 Lay out 3 paper plates. Divide the 12 pieces of pizza equally among 3 people (in thirds).

3 Lay out 4 paper plates. Divide the 12 pieces of pizza equally among 4 people (in fourths).

4 Lay out 6 paper plates. Divide the 12 pieces of pizza equally among 6 people (in sixths).

 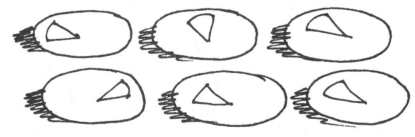 

Divide the pizza among 8 people. Glue the pieces of pizza on a piece of paper to show how you gave each person a fair share.

Instant Math Centers • 2–3 © 2000 Creative Teaching Press

Pizza

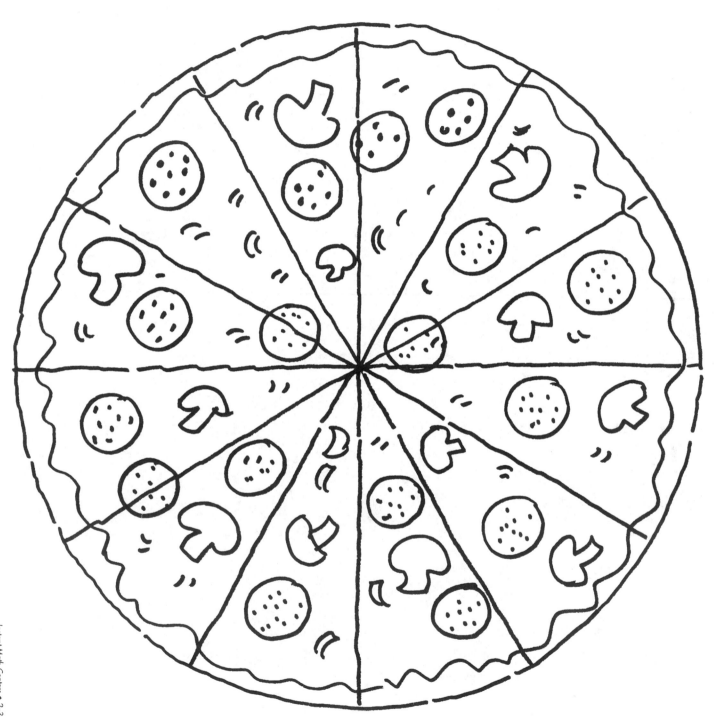

Instant Math Centers • 2-3 © 2000 Creative Teaching Press

Fractions

Geometry

These center activities focus on basic geometric concepts. Students explore the names and properties of geometric shapes, build symmetrical designs, and create congruent figures.

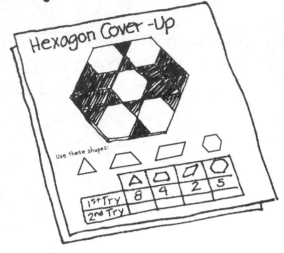

Hexagon Cover-Up
Teaching Tips and Extensions

- Remind students to use only the four pattern block shapes outlined on the activity sheet.
- If you do not have pattern blocks, trace and cut out (or photocopy) each of the four shapes used in this activity on a different color of construction paper. Each student will need several sets of these shapes.

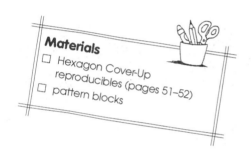

Materials
- ☐ Hexagon Cover-Up reproducibles (pages 51–52)
- ☐ pattern blocks

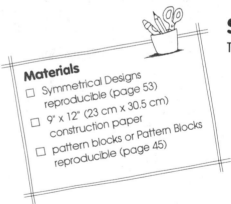

Materials
- ☐ Symmetrical Designs reproducible (page 53)
- ☐ 9" x 12" (23 cm x 30.5 cm) construction paper
- ☐ pattern blocks or Pattern Blocks reproducible (page 45)

Symmetrical Designs
Teaching Tips and Extensions

- ☆ Fold the construction paper in half, and draw a heavy line on the fold.
- If you do not have pattern blocks, trace and cut out (or photocopy) each shape on a different color of construction paper. Each student will need several sets of these shapes.
- Discuss the definition of *symmetry* and *line of symmetry*.

Congruent Shapes
Teaching Tips and Extensions

- Before introducing this activity, discuss the definition of *congruence*.
- Have students cut out the shapes and match them to prove they are congruent.

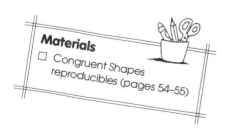

Materials
- ☐ Congruent Shapes reproducibles (pages 54–55)

Hexagon Cover-Up

 Use pattern blocks to completely cover the large hexagon on your Hexagon Cover-Up sheet.

 Fill in the chart to show how many of each shape you used.

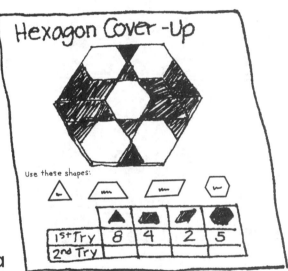

 Cover the hexagon again using a different combination of shapes. Chart your work.

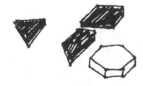
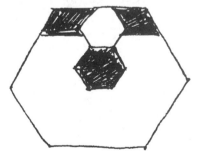

 Use pattern blocks to build the hexagon without using your sheet. Try a different combination of blocks than you used for steps 1–3.

Geometry

Instant Math Centers • 2–3 © 2000 Creative Teaching Press

Name _____

Hexagon Cover-Up

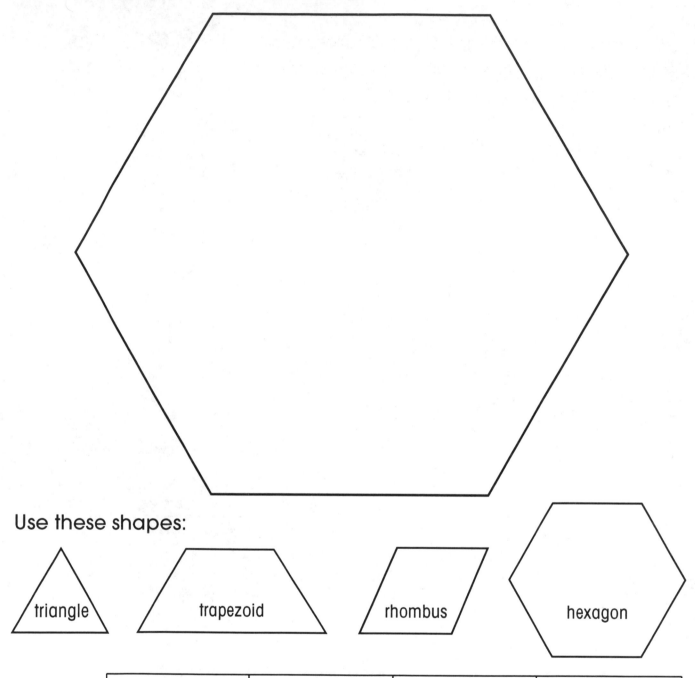

Use these shapes:

triangle trapezoid rhombus hexagon

	▲	⬛▲	◆	⬡
1st Try				
2nd Try				

Instant Math Centers • 2–3 © 2000 Creative Teaching Press

Symmetrical Designs

1 Work with a partner. Use pattern blocks to create a design on one side of a folded sheet of paper. Start the design on the fold.

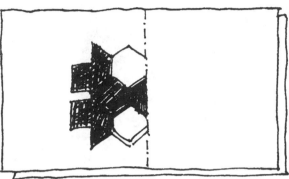

2 Invite your partner to create a symmetrical design on the other side of the fold line.

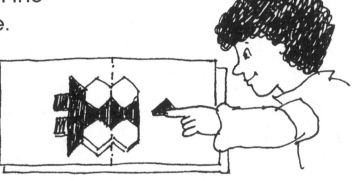

3 Trade places and repeat the activity several times.

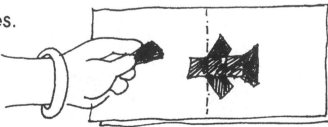

Instant Math Centers • 2–3 © 2000 Creative Teaching Press

Challenge Find 5 objects in the classroom that are symmetrical. Sketch each object and draw in the line of symmetry on a sheet of paper.

Geometry

Congruent Shapes

1 Work with a partner. On a Dot Paper sheet, connect dots to make a closed shape of your choice.

2 Invite your partner to make a congruent shape on a separate Dot Paper sheet. It must be the exact same shape and size.

3 Take turns and repeat the activity 5 times.

Challenge Find 5 congruent shapes in your classroom. Draw each shape on a separate sheet and name the objects.

Name _____

Dot Paper

Instant Math Centers • 2–3 © 2000 Creative Teaching Press

Geometry

Graphing

Graphing is a way to organize and analyze information. When students are involved in collecting and organizing the information, graphing experiences become more meaningful. These center activities help students begin with concrete graphs made with real objects and progress to picture graphs and symbolic graphs. Reading and summarizing the information displayed is an important final step.

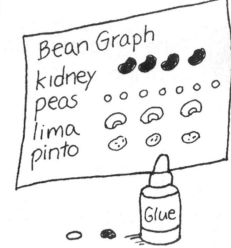

Materials
- ☐ Bean Graph reproducibles (pages 57–58)
- ☐ 2–3 pkgs. mixed dried beans in a bowl
- ☐ chart paper
- ☐ small scoop
- ☐ construction paper
- ☐ glue

Bean Graph
Teaching Tips and Extensions
☆ Label each type of bean on a chart, and place it at the center.

● If mixed beans are unavailable, purchase different kinds of beans and peas and mix them together.

● A small scoop used for measuring coffee or a 35-mm film canister works well.

Color Cube Graph
Teaching Tips and Extensions
● Although linking cubes are suggested, any small cubes or counters in a variety of colors may be used.

● The size of the cup you select will depend on the size of the manipulatives. Choose a cup that is large enough to select a representative sample of cubes.

● Use 1" (2.5 cm) graph paper instead of the Graph Paper reproducible (page 60).

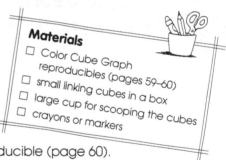

Materials
- ☐ Color Cube Graph reproducibles (pages 59–60)
- ☐ small linking cubes in a box
- ☐ large cup for scooping the cubes
- ☐ crayons or markers

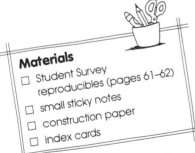

Materials
- ☐ Student Survey reproducibles (pages 61–62)
- ☐ small sticky notes
- ☐ construction paper
- ☐ index cards

Student Survey
Teaching Tips and Extensions
☆ Photocopy and cut apart a few sets of survey cards. Each student will use one card.

● Instead of sticky notes, students could use 1" (2.5 cm) squares of paper and glue them on the graph.

Graphing Bags
Teaching Tips and Extensions
☆ Place 20–25 objects for students to classify in each bag. Bags may contain different types of pasta, beans, shells, keys, buttons, and other small objects. Label each bag.

● Homework Idea: Ask students to make a graphing bag to add to the center.

Materials
- ☐ Graphing Bags reproducibles (pages 63–64 & 60)
- ☐ large assortment of small objects, mixed and bagged
- ☐ resealable plastic bags

Bean Graph

1 Take 1 scoop of beans from the bowl.

2 Sort the beans on construction paper.

3 Glue the beans on the paper and label your graph.

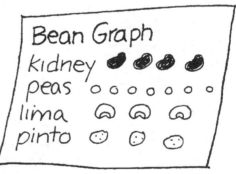

Bean Graph
kidney
peas
lima
pinto

4 Compare your graph to a classmate's.

Math Journal What information does your bean graph show? Write 4 or 5 facts about your graph on your journal page.

Instant! Math Centers • 2–3 © 2000 Creative Teaching Press

Math Journal

What information does your bean graph show?
Write 4 or 5 facts about your graph.

_____

_____

_____

_____

_____

_____

_____

_____

_____

_____

_____

_____

_____

_____

Instant Math Centers • 2–3 © 2000 Creative Teaching Press

Color Cube Graph

1 Scoop a cupful of cubes from the container.

2 Arrange the cubes by color to form a bar graph.

3 Record your graph on your Graph Paper sheet by coloring in 1 square for each cube in the graph. Use matching colors.

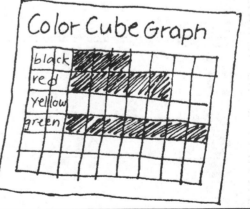

Color Cube Graph

black						
red						
yellow						
green						

Challenge Make a graph that shows the hair color of all of your classmates on another sheet.

Instant Math Centers • 2–3 © 2000 Creative Teaching Press

Graphing

Color Cube Graph

Name _____

Instant Math Centers • 2–3 © 2000 Creative Teaching Press

Student Survey

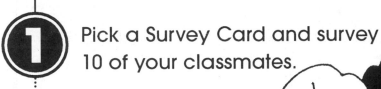

1 Pick a Survey Card and survey 10 of your classmates.

2 Record the answers with tally marks on your Survey Card.

3 Use sticky notes (or paper squares) to make a graph of your classmates' answers on a piece of construction paper. Label the graph.

Write your own survey questions on index cards. Give 3 or 4 choices for responses. Survey 10 of your classmates and make a graph of their answers.

Instant Math Centers • 2–3 © 2000 Creative Teaching Press

Graphing

Survey Cards

Which color do you
like best?

red _____

blue _____

yellow _____

Which ice cream flavor
do you like best?

vanilla _____

chocolate _____

strawberry _____

What color are
your eyes?

brown _____

green _____

blue _____

hazel _____

gray _____

What is your
favorite season?

winter _____

spring _____

summer _____

fall _____

How did you get
to school today?

walk _____

car _____

bus _____

bike _____

What kind of shoes
are you wearing?

tennis shoes _____

sandals _____

other _____

Instant Math Centers • 2–3 © 2000 Creative Teaching Press

Graphing Bags

1 Choose a graphing bag. Sort the objects into several categories.

2 Use your Graphing Grid sheet to graph the items in the bag.

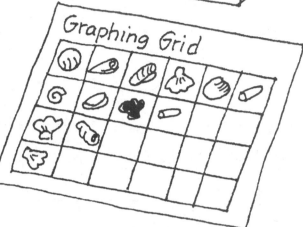

3 Write 2 statements about the graph on a piece of paper.

4 Choose another bag and make another graph on another sheet. Write 2 new statements on a piece of paper.

 Use a Graph Paper sheet to show 1 of your graphs in bar graph form. Label the bar graph.

Instant Math Centers • 2–3 © 2000 Creative Teaching Press

Graphing

Graphing Grid

64

Instant Math Centers • 2–3 © 2000 Creative Teaching Press

Logic

These center activities require logical thinking in order to reach solutions. Students must organize information and think through several steps of a process to determine the outcome. By encouraging students to talk or write about their experiences, they become conscious of effective problem-solving strategies.

Fill It In

Teaching Tips and Extensions

- Have students use two different colors of paper squares or linking cubes instead of coloring on the game board.

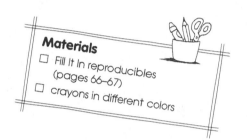

Materials
- ☐ Fill It In reproducibles (pages 66–67)
- ☐ crayons in different colors

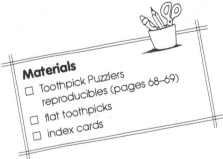

Materials
- ☐ Toothpick Puzzlers reproducibles (pages 68–69)
- ☐ flat toothpicks
- ☐ index cards

Toothpick Puzzlers

Teaching Tips and Extensions

- ☆ Photocopy, cut apart, and laminate the Toothpick Puzzler cards.
- Let students use rulers to create giant-sized puzzles on butcher paper.

Show the Ways

Teaching Tips and Extensions

- Answer Key: There are 6 ways to seat 3 students in a row. There are 10 ways to combine 3 flavors of ice cream. There are 12 ways to seat 4 passengers in a car.
- Have students work in pairs.
- Instead of using different-colored manipulatives, prepare cards to represent the variables in each problem.

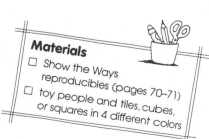

Materials
- ☐ Show the Ways reproducibles (pages 70–71)
- ☐ toy people and tiles, cubes, or squares in 4 different colors

Fill It In

1  Play with a partner. Each player needs a different color crayon.

2 Use the game board and take turns coloring in either 1 square or 2 squares with a common side. The player who colors in the last square is the winner.

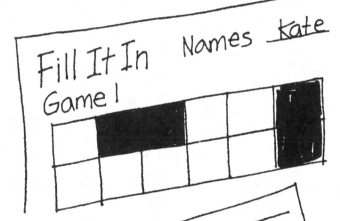

3 Play 5 more times. Think about the strategies you are using.

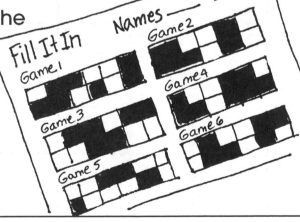

 **Challenge** Think together with your partner to explain strategies for winning Fill It In. Write your strategies on the back of your sheet.

Instant Math Centers • 2–3 © 2000 Creative Teaching Press

Fill It In

Names _____

Game 1

Game 2

Game 3

Game 4

Game 5

Game 6

Instant Math Centers • 2–3 © 2000 Creative Teaching Press

Logic

Toothpick Puzzlers

1 Select a Toothpick Puzzler card.

2 Use the correct number of toothpicks to build the design on the card. Build the design on a piece of paper. Follow the directions on the card to solve the puzzle.

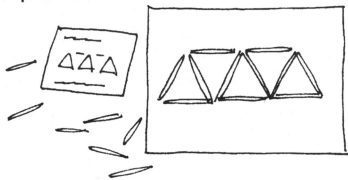

3 Choose new cards. Try to solve all 8 puzzles.

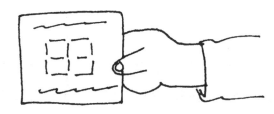

Challenge

Invent a "Toothpick Puzzler" card of your own. Draw the design and write the directions on an index card. Have a classmate try to solve your puzzle.

Instant Math Centers • 2–3 © 2000 Creative Teaching Press

Toothpick Puzzlers

1. Arrange 9 toothpicks like this:

Take away 3 toothpicks so that only 1 triangle is left.

2. Arrange 11 toothpicks like this:

Take away 1 toothpick so that 4 triangles are left.

3. Arrange 13 toothpicks like this:

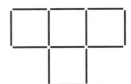

Take away 1 toothpick so that 3 equal squares are left.

4. Arrange 12 toothpicks like this:

Take away 4 toothpicks so that 2 equal squares are left.

5. Arrange 10 toothpicks like this:

Move 5 toothpicks so that only 1 rectangle is left.

6. Arrange 10 toothpicks like this:

Move 2 toothpicks so that 3 equal squares are left.

7. Arrange 9 toothpicks like this:

Take away 3 toothpicks so that 2 equal triangles are left.

8. Arrange 13 toothpicks like this:

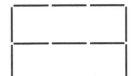

Move 2 toothpicks so that 3 squares are left.

Possible Solutions (Fold back or cut off before reproducing.)

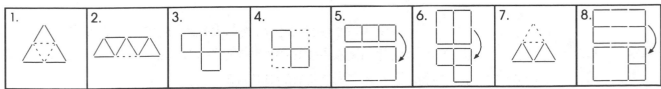

Instant Math Centers • 2-3 © 2000 Creative Teaching Press

Logic

Show the Ways

Use manipulatives of different colors to work out the solutions to the following problems:

1 Show all the different ways Sue, Janet, and Dave can be seated together in one row at the movies. Record your solution on your Show the Ways sheet.

2 Show all the different triple-scoop combinations you can make using scoops of chocolate, vanilla, and strawberry ice cream. Record your solution on your sheet.

3 Show all the different ways you can seat 4 passengers in a car if 2 sit in the front and 2 sit in the back. Draw your solution on the back of your sheet.

Challenge How many ways can you arrange 5 books on a shelf? Draw all the possibilities on a piece of paper.

Instant Math Centers • 2–3 © 2000 Creative Teaching Press

Show the Ways

1. Record all the ways Sue, Janet, and Dave could be seated together in a row at the movies.

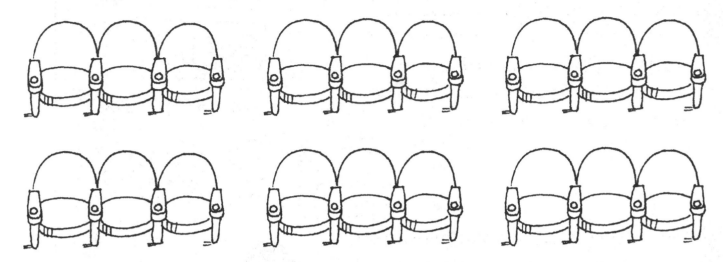

2. Record all the triple-scoop combinations you can make using scoops of chocolate, vanilla, and strawberry ice cream.

3. On the back of this page, draw all the ways you can seat 4 passengers in a car if 2 sit in the front and 2 sit in the back.

Instant Math Centers • 2–3 © 2000 Creative Teaching Press

Logic

Measurement

Students will enjoy these exploratory center activities as they estimate, measure, and compare, using a variety of both nonstandard and standard units of measurement. These activities offer students experiences in measuring capacity, length, and weight.

Materials
- [ ] Different Shapes—Different Levels reproducibles (pages 73–74)
- [ ] several cups of rice in a flat container
- [ ] 5 containers of different shapes and sizes, labeled A, B, C, D, E
- [ ] measuring cups
- [ ] erasable marking pens or grease pencils
- [ ] funnels
- [ ] cloth for wiping off pen or pencil marks

Different Shapes—Different Levels
Teaching Tips and Extensions
- Show students how to measure exactly one cup of rice by filling it and smoothing the top.
- Show how to use the funnel for narrow-mouthed containers.

Which Is More?
Teaching Tips and Extensions
- Show students how to use the funnel for narrow-mouthed containers.
- Encourage students to explain their predictions of which containers will hold more.

Materials
- [ ] Which Is More? reproducibles (pages 75–76)
- [ ] 5 containers of different shapes and sizes, labeled A, B, C, D, E
- [ ] several cups of rice in a flat container
- [ ] measuring cups
- [ ] funnels

Materials
- [ ] How Many Cubes? reproducibles (pages 77–78)
- [ ] pencils, books, student desk and chair for measuring
- [ ] linking cubes

How Many Cubes?
Teaching Tips and Extensions
- Make sure students understand that the difference between their estimate and the actual measurement goes in the *Difference* column on their How Many Cubes? activity sheet.

Weighing a Pound

Materials
- [ ] Weighing a Pound reproducible (page 79)
- [ ] containers of beans, popcorn, rice, and other food items to weigh
- [ ] small scoops
- [ ] sturdy resealable plastic bags
- [ ] balance scales
- [ ] 1-lb. (½-kg) weights

Lightest to Heaviest
Materials
- [ ] Lightest to Heaviest reproducibles (pages 80–81)
- [ ] book, box of crayons, shoe, clay, stapler, and other objects to weigh, ranging from 1 ounce (28 g) to 2 pounds (1 kg)
- [ ] balance scales
- [ ] various weights, ranging from 1 ounce (28 g) to 2 pounds (1 kg)

Different Shapes—Different Levels

1 Fill a measuring cup with rice. Choose a container. Use a marking pen to show how high you think the rice will be when you pour it into the container.

2 Use a funnel to pour the cup of rice into the container. Compare the actual height of the rice to your guess.

3 Wipe the marker line off the container and repeat the activity with the other containers.

 On your journal page, describe how the shape and size of the container affect the level of the rice.

Instant Math Centers • 2–3 © 2000 Creative Teaching Press

Measurement

Name _____

Math Journal

Describe how the shape and size of the container affect the level of the rice.

_____

_____

_____

_____

_____

_____

_____

_____

_____

_____

_____

_____

_____

_____

_____

_____

_____

Instant Math Centers • 2–3 © 2000 Creative Teaching Press

Which Is More?

1 Arrange the containers in order from smallest capacity to largest capacity. Write your prediction on your Which Is More? sheet.

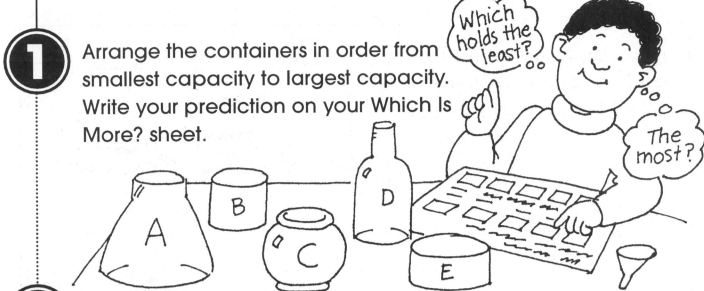

2 Use a measuring cup to find out how many cups of rice each container holds. Write the actual capacity of each container on your sheet.

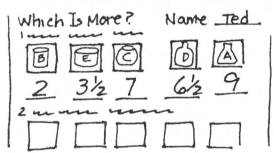

3 Was your guess right? Change the order of the containers if you need to and draw the correct order on your sheet.

Instant Math Centers • 2-3 © 2000 Creative Teaching Press

Challenge Find the total capacity of all 5 containers. Write it on the back of your sheet.

Measurement

Which Is More?

1. Make a prediction. Draw the containers in order from smallest to largest capacity. Write the letter label on each drawing.

SMALLEST → LARGEST

Actual Capacity	Actual Capacity	Actual Capacity	Actual Capacity	Actual Capacity

2. Was your guess right? Change the order of the containers if you need to.

SMALLEST → LARGEST

Instant Math Centers • 2–3 © 2000 Creative Teaching Press

How Many Cubes?

1 Choose an object listed on your How Many Cubes? sheet. Estimate its length (or height) in cubes and write your estimate on your sheet.

2 Measure the object with cubes. Write the actual measurement on your sheet.

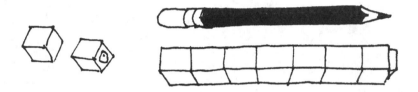

3 How close was your estimate? Write the difference on your sheet.

Name ___Bill___

How Many Cubes?

I Measured	My Estimate	Actual Measurement	Difference
✏	8	7	1

4 Repeat the activity with the other objects on your sheet.

Challenge Find something in the classroom that is 10 cubes long. Find something close to 20 cubes long and something close to 50 cubes long. List what you found on the back of your sheet.

Measurement

Instant Math Centers • 2–3 © 2000 Creative Teaching Press

How Many Cubes?

I Measured	My Estimate	Actual Measurement	Difference
pencil			
book			
my desk			
my chair			
this paper			
a classmate			

Instant Math Centers • 2–3 © 2000 Creative Teaching Press

Weighing a Pound

1 Use a scoop to fill a bag with beans until you think you have 1 pound (¹/₂ kg).

2 Test your estimate on a balance scale. Use the 1-pound (¹/₂-kg) weight.

3 Add or remove beans until you have exactly 1 pound (¹/₂ kg).

4 Repeat the activity several more times. Weigh a different food item each time.

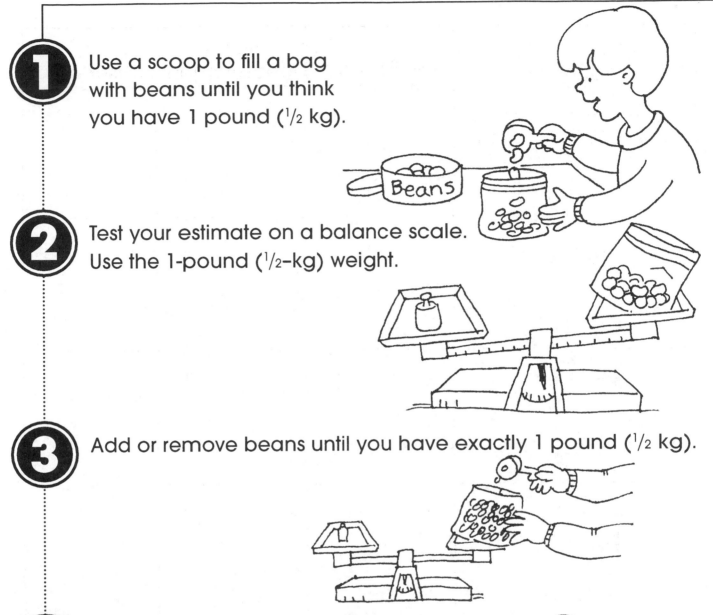

 **Challenge** Find 3 classroom objects that weigh close to 1 pound (¹/₂ kg) each.

Instant Math Centers • 2–3 © 2000 Creative Teaching Press

Measurement

Lightest to Heaviest

1 Select 5 objects. Use your best estimate to place them in order from lightest to heaviest.

2 Draw the objects in order on your Lightest to Heaviest sheet.

3 Use a balance scale and weights to weigh all 5 objects.

4 Write the actual weight of each object. Draw the objects again in correct order from lightest to heaviest on your sheet.

Challenge Pick 5 different objects from the classroom. See if a partner can order them from lightest to heaviest. Use the scale and weights to check the estimate.

Instant Math Centers • 2–3 © 2000 Creative Teaching Press

Lightest to Heaviest

Name _____

My Estimate	Actual Weight
LIGHTEST ↓ **HEAVIEST**	
1.	1. Weight _____
2.	2. Weight _____
3.	3. Weight _____
4.	4. Weight _____
5.	5. Weight _____

Money

Your students will have fun learning more about money as they work with these center activities. The focus is to give students many experiences in counting, grouping, and exchanging coins. Students will benefit most by using real coins as they work.

How Many Ways?
Teaching Tips and Extensions

☆ Make many copies of the Coins reproducible, cut apart the coins, and store them in a separate divided container.

● Extend the activity by changing the amount to $5.00, $10.00, or $25.00. Provide students with $1.00, $5.00, and $10.00 bills in play money, and have students draw the bills on their paper.

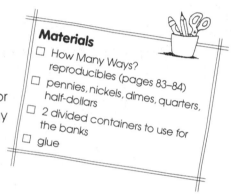

Materials
- ☐ How Many Ways? reproducibles (pages 83–84)
- ☐ pennies, nickels, dimes, quarters, half-dollars
- ☐ 2 divided containers to use for the banks
- ☐ glue

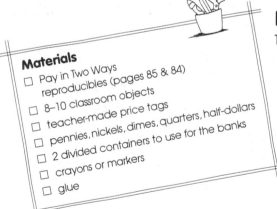

Materials
- ☐ Pay in Two Ways reproducibles (pages 85 & 84)
- ☐ 8–10 classroom objects
- ☐ teacher-made price tags
- ☐ pennies, nickels, dimes, quarters, half-dollars
- ☐ 2 divided containers to use for the banks
- ☐ crayons or markers
- ☐ glue

Pay in Two Ways
Teaching Tips and Extensions

☆ Make many copies of the Coins reproducible, cut apart the coins, and store them in a separate divided container.

☆ Tape a price tag on each object. Start with prices less than $1.00 each. As students gain in skill, increase the price of each object and the amount of money each student has to shop with.

Toy Store
Teaching Tips and Extensions

☆ Make several copies of the Toy Store reproducible on page 87. Cut apart the cards, and laminate them.

● Cut several sheets of green construction paper into rectangles the size of a dollar bill. Label each bill $10.00, $5.00, or $1.00.

● As students gain in experience, increase the price of the objects on the Toy Store reproducible, and have students start with a $20.00 bill.

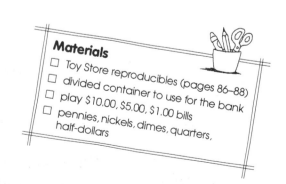

Materials
- ☐ Toy Store reproducibles (pages 86–88)
- ☐ divided container to use for the bank
- ☐ play $10.00, $5.00, $1.00 bills
- ☐ pennies, nickels, dimes, quarters, half-dollars

How Many Ways?

1 Use the coins to show 25¢ as many ways as you can.

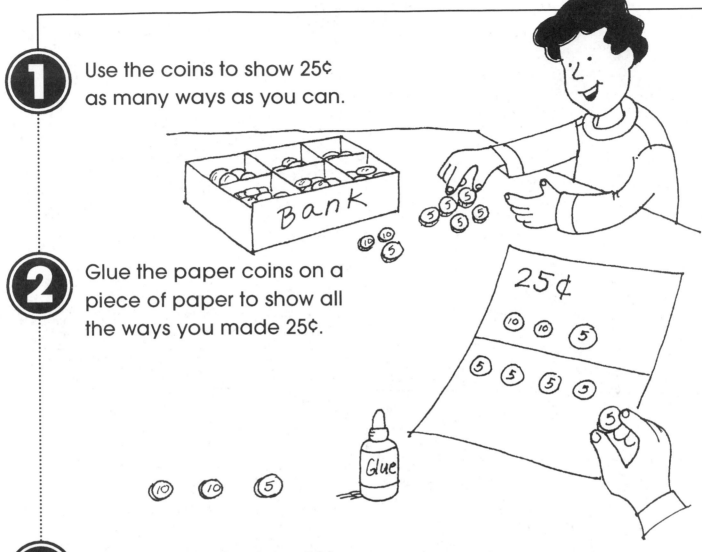

2 Glue the paper coins on a piece of paper to show all the ways you made 25¢.

3 Use the coins to show 50¢ as many ways as you can. Glue the paper coins on your paper to show all the ways you made 50¢.

Challenge Work with a partner. Use coins to show $1.00 as many ways as you can. Glue the paper coins on your paper to show all the ways you made $1.00.

Instant Math Centers • 2-3 @ 2000 Creative Teaching Press

Money

Coins

Pay in Two Ways

1 Select an item.

2 Count out the coins needed to pay for the item. Draw the item and write its price on a piece of paper. Glue paper coins on your paper to show how you paid for the item.

3 Count out a different combination of coins to pay for the item. Glue paper coins to show how you paid.

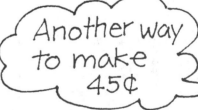

Another way to make 45¢

4 Repeat the activity 4 more times. Select a different item each time and pay for it in 2 different ways. Glue paper coins on your paper to show how you paid each time.

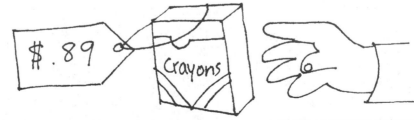

Challenge Pretend you are using a $1.00 bill to pay for each item. Figure out the change you would get from each purchase. Show your work on your paper.

Instant Math Centers • 2-3 © 2000 Creative Teaching Press

Money

Toy Store

1 Work with a partner, taking turns. Start with a $10.00 bill.

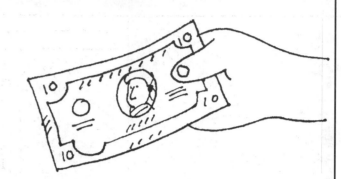

2 Pick a card and subtract the price of the toy from the $10.00. Trade in bills and coins at the bank when necessary.

3 Keep selecting cards and paying the bank until you run out of money. Partners should check each other's work.

Math Journal Describe some of the trades you made to pay the bank on your journal page.

Instant Math Centers • 2–3 © 2000 Creative Teaching Press

Toy Store

Instant Math Centers • 2–3 © 2000 Creative Teaching Press

Money

Math Journal

Describe some of the trades you made to pay the bank.

_____

_____

_____

_____

_____

_____

_____

_____

_____

_____

_____

_____

_____

_____

_____

Instant Math Centers • 2–3 © 2000 Creative Teaching Press

Multiplication

These center activities offer hands-on, beginning multiplication experiences that include making equal groups, constructing arrays, and recording multiplication problems in various ways. They provide students with concrete experiences that help them to build a foundation for understanding multiplication.

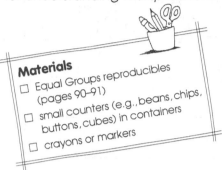

Materials
- ☐ Equal Groups reproducibles (pages 90–91)
- ☐ small counters (e.g., beans, chips, buttons, cubes) in containers
- ☐ crayons or markers

Equal Groups
Teaching Tips and Extensions

- Students do not need to use all 25 counters when creating the equal groups. For example, they could use 18 counters to make 3 groups of 6.
- Introduce the activity by reading aloud *What Comes in Twos, Threes, and Fours* by Suzanne Aker.

Multiplication Designs
Teaching Tips and Extensions

- Show students how to label equal groups with words, with an addition equation, and as a multiplication problem.

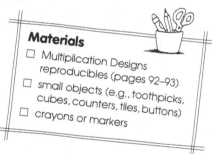

Materials
- ☐ Multiplication Designs reproducibles (pages 92–93)
- ☐ small objects (e.g., toothpicks, cubes, counters, tiles, buttons)
- ☐ crayons or markers

Materials
- ☐ Multiplication Arrays reproducibles (pages 94–95)
- ☐ several sets of teacher-made number cards
- ☐ colored tiles or 1" (2.5 cm) squares of colored paper
- ☐ crayons or markers

Multiplication Arrays
Teaching Tips and Extensions

- ☆ Make sets of 6–8 number cards using multiplication products that would be appropriate for your students. Increase the difficulty level as students' skills progress.
- Use 1" (2.5 cm) graph paper instead of the Graph Paper reproducible (page 95).

Under the Sea Multiplication
Teaching Tips and Extensions

- ☆ Photocopy the sea creature cards, and cut them apart. Place the cards for each sea creature in a separate envelope. Glue one picture on the front of each envelope, and label each one.
- Discuss the attributes of the creatures with the class (e.g., 8 legs on the octopus, 2 claws on the lobster).
- Have students practice writing sentences with words and numbers. For example, *One turtle has 4 legs. Three turtles have 12 legs. 3 x 4 = 12.*
- Introduce the activity by reading aloud *Sea Squares* by Joy Hulme.

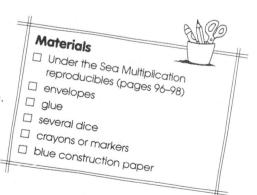

Materials
- ☐ Under the Sea Multiplication reproducibles (pages 96–98)
- ☐ envelopes
- ☐ glue
- ☐ several dice
- ☐ crayons or markers
- ☐ blue construction paper

Equal Groups

1 Start with 25 counters. Arrange them into equal groups, such as 5 in a group or 3 in a group. Use some or all of the counters.

2 Draw and describe your groups on your Equal Groups sheet as shown. Use words and pictures.

3 Repeat the activity 3 more times. Use a different number of counters each time in the equal groups.

 **Challenge** How many ways can you divide 36 counters into equal groups? Write your answers on the back of your sheet and show them to a classmate.

Instant Math Centers • 2–3 © 2000 Creative Teaching Press

Equal Groups

Name _____

Groups of _____

Groups of _____

Groups of _____

Groups of _____

Multiplication Designs

1 Use 1 set of objects to make a design arranged in equal groups.

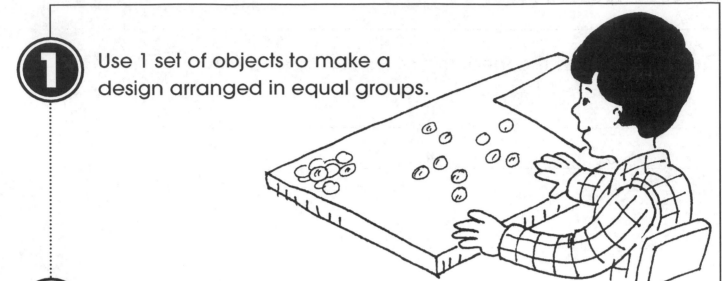

2 Draw a picture of your design on a piece of paper and label it 3 different ways as shown.

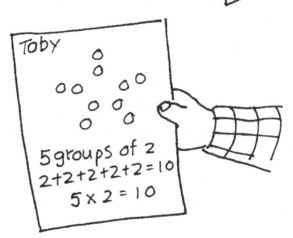

Toby

5 groups of 2
2+2+2+2+2=10
5 × 2 = 10

3 Repeat the activity at least 3 times. Use a different set of objects each time.

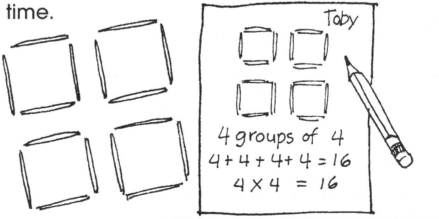

Toby

4 groups of 4
4 + 4 + 4 + 4 = 16
4 × 4 = 16

Math Journal Explain in words the meaning of 3 x 5 = 15 on your journal page.

Instant Math Centers • 2–3 © 2000 Creative Teaching Press

Math Journal

Explain in words the meaning of 3 x 5 = 15.

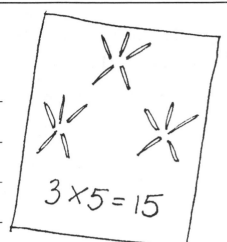

3 x 5 = 15

Instant Math Centers • 2–3 © 2000 Creative Teaching Press

Multiplication Arrays

1 Select a number card and take that number of colored tiles. Use the tiles to make an array on your Graph Paper sheet.

2 Color in squares on your sheet to make a record of the array. Write the multiplication problem, too.

3 Pick 5 new number cards and repeat the activity for each number.

Challenge Work with a partner. Pick a number and use tiles to make all possible arrays for that number. Think of another number that has even more possible arrays.

Instant Math Centers • 2–3 © 2000 Creative Teaching Press

Graph Paper

Instant Math Centers • 2-3 © 2000 Creative Teaching Press

Multiplication

Under the Sea Multiplication

1 Select a sea creature envelope.

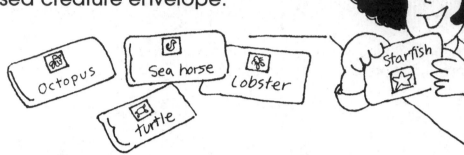

2 Roll a die and take that many sea creatures from the envelope. Color the creatures.

3 Glue the pictures on the blue paper. Write a multiplication sentence to go with the pictures.

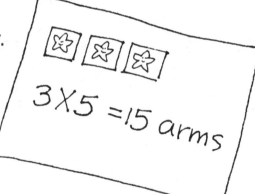

$$3 \times 5 = 15 \text{ arms}$$

4 Repeat the activity at least 3 more times with other sea creatures.

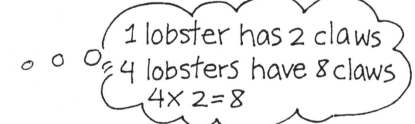

1 lobster has 2 claws
4 lobsters have 8 claws
$4 \times 2 = 8$

Math Journal Work with a partner. Make lists of things that come in multiples of 2, 3, 4, and 5 on your journal page.

Instant Math Centers • 2–3 © 2000 Creative Teaching Press

Sea Creatures

starfish 5 arms	starfish 5 arms	starfish 5 arms	starfish 5 arms	starfish 5 arms
octopus 8 tentacles	octopus 8 tentacles	octopus 8 tentacles	octopus 8 tentacles	octopus 8 tentacles
lobster 2 claws	lobster 2 claws	lobster 2 claws	lobster 2 claws	lobster 2 claws
sea horse 1 tail	sea horse 1 tail	sea horse 1 tail	sea horse 1 tail	sea horse 1 tail
turtle 4 legs	turtle 4 legs	turtle 4 legs	turtle 4 legs	turtle 4 legs

Instant Math Centers • 2–3 © 2000 Creative Teaching Press

Multiplication

Math Journal

Work with a partner. Make lists of things that come in multiples of 2, 3, 4, and 5.

_____

_____

_____

_____

_____

_____

_____

_____

_____

_____

_____

_____

Instant Math Centers • 2–3 © 2000 Creative Teaching Press

Place Value

To understand place value, students need many experiences counting, grouping, and trading concrete objects to form hundreds, tens, and ones. Display the corresponding symbols so students see the connection between their manipulatives and the numerals. These center activities will help students develop an understanding of place value to 9999.

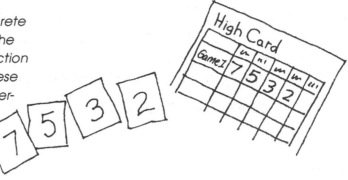

Building Numbers
Teaching Tips and Extensions
- If base ten blocks are not available, photocopy the Base Ten Blocks reproducibles (pages 101-102) on tagboard or construction paper. Cut apart the hundreds, tens, and ones, and store them at the center. Each pair of students will need at least 9 hundreds, 9 tens, and 9 ones.
- See if students can make a generalization about how many different numbers can be made with three cards.

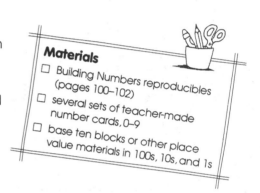

Materials
- ☐ Building Numbers reproducibles (pages 100–102)
- ☐ several sets of teacher-made number cards, 0–9
- ☐ base ten blocks or other place value materials in 100s, 10s, and 1s

Place Value Pictures
Teaching Tips and Extensions
- If base ten blocks are not available, photocopy the Base Ten Blocks reproducibles (pages 101-102) on tagboard or construction paper. Cut apart the hundreds, tens, and ones, and store them at the center. Each pair of students will need at least 9 hundreds, 9 tens, and 9 ones.
- Discuss how students can make exchanges when doing the Challenge activity (e.g., they can trade 1 ten block for 10 ones).

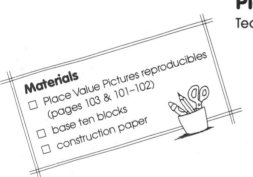

Materials
- ☐ Place Value Pictures reproducibles (pages 103 & 101–102)
- ☐ base ten blocks
- ☐ construction paper

High Card
Teaching Tips and Extensions
- ☆ Place two sets of number cards in each bag.
- Vary the game by setting the goal to make the smallest number each time.

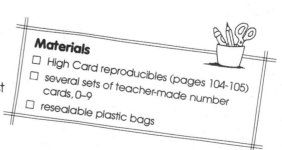

Materials
- ☐ High Card reproducibles (pages 104–105)
- ☐ several sets of teacher-made number cards, 0–9
- ☐ resealable plastic bags

Building Numbers

1 Work with a partner. Pick 3 cards and arrange them to show a 3-digit number.

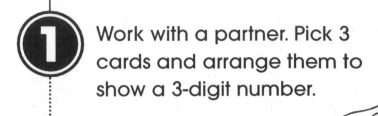

2 Have your partner use base ten blocks to build the number showing ones, tens, and hundreds.

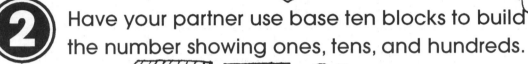

3 Use the same 3 cards. Take turns making new numbers and building the numbers with base ten blocks.

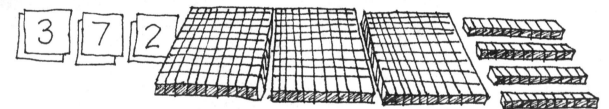

4 When no new numbers can be made, pick 3 new cards and play again.

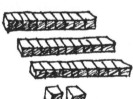

Challenge Pick 3 new cards and make a 3-digit number. Find as many different ways as you can to build the number using base ten blocks.

Instant Math Centers • 2-3 © 2000 Creative Teaching Press

Base Ten Blocks (A)

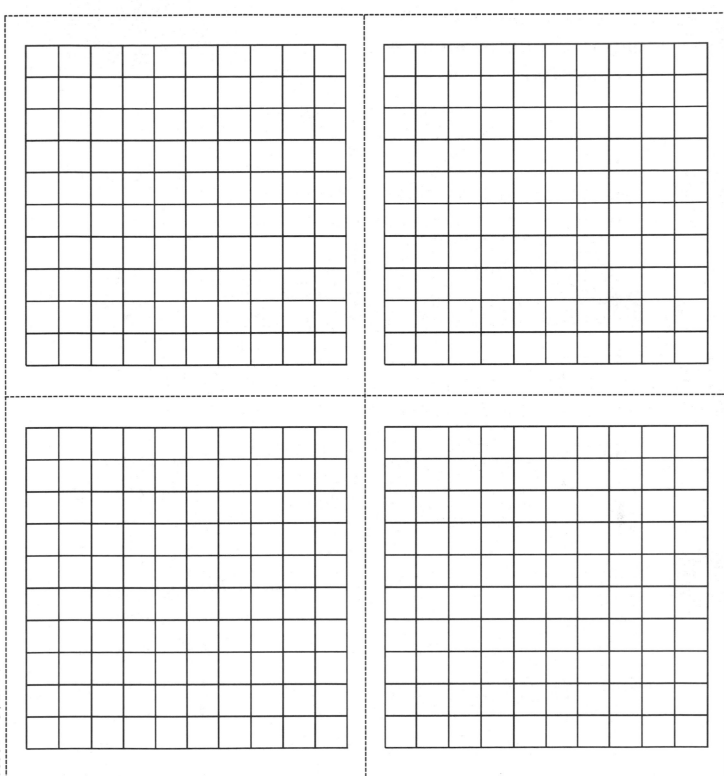

Instant Math Centers • 2–3 © 2000 Creative Teaching Press

Place Value

Base Ten Blocks (B)

Instant Math Centers • 2–3 © 2000 Creative Teaching Press

Place Value Pictures

1 Use base ten blocks to make a picture or design on a piece of paper.

2 Trace around the blocks (or cut and paste paper base ten blocks) to make a recording of your picture.

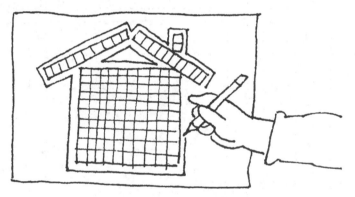

3 Record the value of each base ten block. Then add up all the hundreds, tens, and ones to find the total value of your picture.

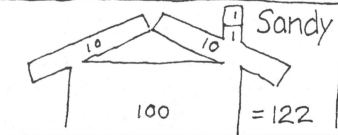

 **Challenge** Exchange pictures with a partner. Use base ten blocks to build a new picture that is the same value as your partner's picture.

Instant Math Centers • 2–3 © 2000 Creative Teaching Press

Place Value

High Card

1 Play with a partner. The object is to make the largest number. Empty a bag of number cards. Shuffle the cards and place them facedown.

2 Pick 4 cards. Arrange them in any order you want to make a 4-digit number. Write your number on your High Card sheet beside Game 1.

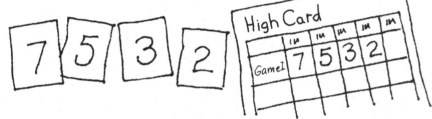

3 Now it is your partner's turn to do step 2.

4 Compare your numbers. Whoever has the larger number checks the winner's box. Play High Card 7 more times.

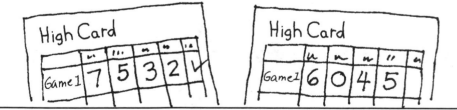

Challenge Explain your strategies for making the largest number. How will it change if the object is to make the smallest number? Write your answers on the back of your sheet.

Instant Math Centers • 2–3 © 2000 Creative Teaching Press

Name _____

High Card

	Thousands 1000s	Hundreds 100s	Tens 10s	Ones 1s	Winner
Game 1	_____ ,	_____	_____	_____	
Game 2	_____ ,	_____	_____	_____	
Game 3	_____ ,	_____	_____	_____	
Game 4	_____ ,	_____	_____	_____	
Game 5	_____ ,	_____	_____	_____	
Game 6	_____ ,	_____	_____	_____	
Game 7	_____ ,	_____	_____	_____	
Game 8	_____ ,	_____	_____	_____	

Instant Math Centers • 2–3 © 2000 Creative Teaching Press

Place Value

Probability

These center activities offer students opportunities to explore concepts of chance. Students will collect and organize data, predict outcomes, and check their predictions.

Guess the Colors
Teaching Tips and Extensions

☆ Place one red cube and two blue cubes in each paper bag.

● If you do not have colored cubes, use colored tiles, marbles, or any small red and blue manipulatives.

● Change the proportion or number of cubes in the bag as students progress.

● Ask students to describe their strategies for making predictions.

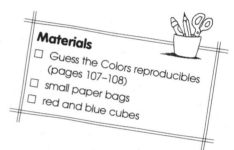

Materials
☐ Guess the Colors reproducibles (pages 107–108)
☐ small paper bags
☐ red and blue cubes

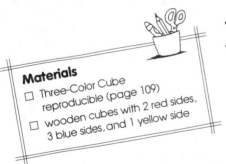

Materials
☐ Three-Color Cube reproducible (page 109)
☐ wooden cubes with 2 red sides, 3 blue sides, and 1 yellow side

Three-Color Cube
Teaching Tips and Extensions

☆ Use paints or permanent markers to color plain wooden cubes, or place colored stickers on cubes or dice.

● Discuss with students the ratio of yellow to red to blue. After students practice with the first cube, change to a cube with a different color ratio.

● Have students post their activity sheets at the center. Compile student data on a class graph.

Heads or Tails
Teaching Tips and Extensions

● For practice, have students guess heads or tails for one coin and record their guesses and actual results. Then, demonstrate and record with two coins. Some students may need to do the independent activity with one coin only.

● Use two-color counters, and have students record the color that comes up each time.

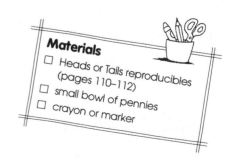

Materials
☐ Heads or Tails reproducibles (pages 110–112)
☐ small bowl of pennies
☐ crayon or marker

Guess the Colors

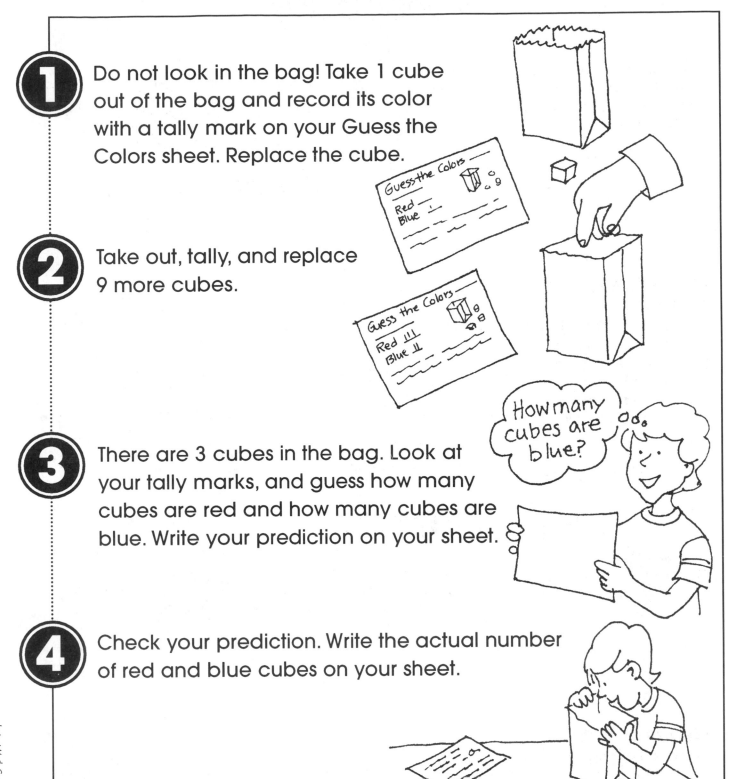

1 Do not look in the bag! Take 1 cube out of the bag and record its color with a tally mark on your Guess the Colors sheet. Replace the cube.

2 Take out, tally, and replace 9 more cubes.

3 There are 3 cubes in the bag. Look at your tally marks, and guess how many cubes are red and how many cubes are blue. Write your prediction on your sheet.

4 Check your prediction. Write the actual number of red and blue cubes on your sheet.

Challenge Ask a classmate to put 4 cubes in the bag. Repeat the activity, but pull out a cube 15 times.

Instant Math Centers • 2–3 © 2000 Creative Teaching Press

Probability

Name _____

Guess the Colors

1. Take out 10 cubes and tally here:

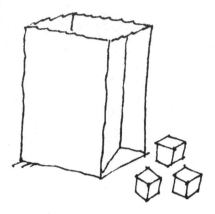

   Red _____

   Blue _____

2. I think there are _____ red and _____ blue cubes in the bag.

3. There are actually _____ red and _____ blue cubes in the bag.

- -

Name _____

Guess the Colors

1. Take out 10 cubes and tally here:

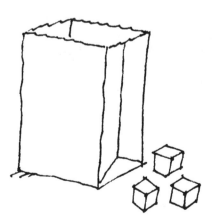

   Red _____

   Blue _____

2. I think there are _____ red and _____ blue cubes in the bag.

3. There are actually _____ red and _____ blue cubes in the bag.

Instant Math Centers • 2–3 © 2000 Creative Teaching Press

Three-Color Cube

1 Look carefully at the colors on the cube. Predict which color will come up most often if you roll the cube 20 times. Predict which color will come up least often. Write your predictions on a piece of paper.

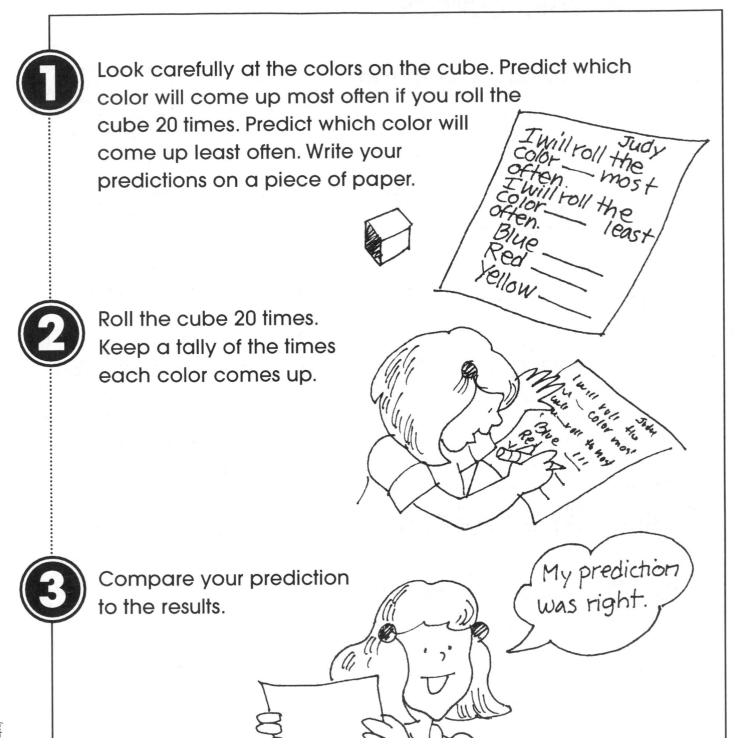

2 Roll the cube 20 times. Keep a tally of the times each color comes up.

3 Compare your prediction to the results.

Instant Math Centers • 2–3 © 2000 Creative Teaching Press

Challenge Work with a partner. Write your predictions, roll the cube 50 times, keep a tally, and compare your results to when you rolled the cube 20 times.

Probability

Heads or Tails

1 If you toss 2 pennies at the same time, what will be the most common way for the pennies to land? Circle your prediction on your Heads or Tails sheet.

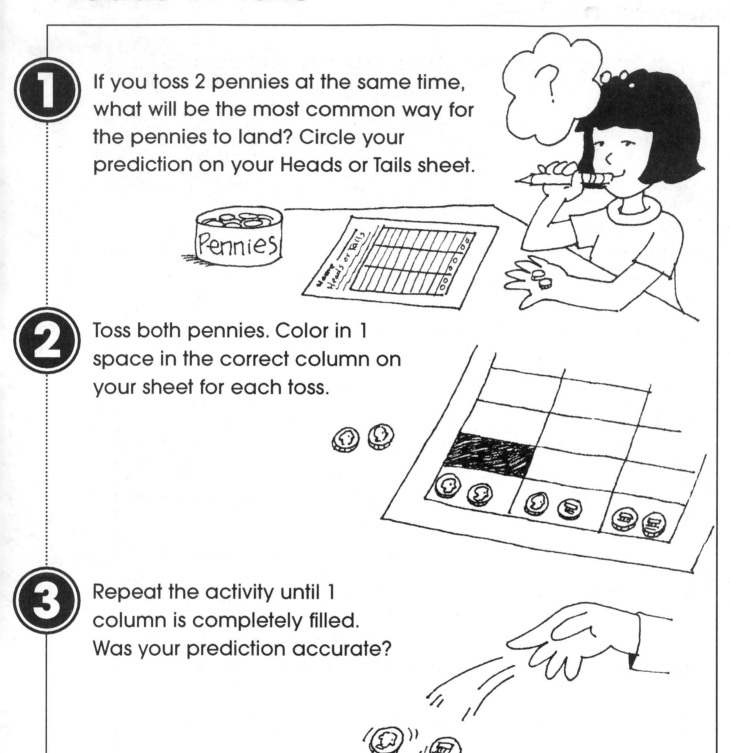

2 Toss both pennies. Color in 1 space in the correct column on your sheet for each toss.

3 Repeat the activity until 1 column is completely filled. Was your prediction accurate?

Math Journal Compare your results to those of other students. Which combination came up most often? Why? Which came up least often? Write about your findings on your journal page.

Instant Math Centers • 2–3 © 2000 Creative Teaching Press

Name _____

Heads or Tails

1. I predict that the pennies will land like this most often (circle one choice):

2. Color in 1 space in the correct column each time you toss the pennies.

Instant Math Centers • 2–3 © 2000 Creative Teaching Press

Probability

Math Journal

Compare your results to those of other students. Which combination came up most often? Why? Which came up least often? Write about your findings.

_____

_____

_____

_____

_____

_____

_____

_____

_____

_____

_____

_____

_____

_____

_____

Instant Math Centers • 2–3 © 2000 Creative Teaching Press

Subtraction

Students need a variety of concrete experiences creating, solving, and recording subtraction problems in order to develop strategies for learning the subtraction facts. These center activities provide practice in subtraction, using two-digit numbers, with and without regrouping.

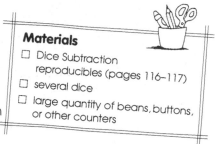

Subtraction Sock

Teaching Tips and Extensions

- Change the number of beans in the sock to focus on a particular set of subtraction facts.
- Have students work in pairs. One student removes beans and the other must tell how many are still in the sock. Both students count the beans in the sock to check the answer.

Materials
- ☐ Subtraction Sock reproducibles (pages 114–115)
- ☐ large quantity of beans
- ☐ several socks

Dice Subtraction

Teaching Tips and Extensions

- Have students work in groups of two or three and take turns rolling the dice, placing the counters, and writing the equations.
- Make number cubes by covering the sides of dice with stick-on labels. Write the numbers 1–6 on the labels.

Materials
- ☐ Dice Subtraction reproducibles (pages 116–117)
- ☐ several dice
- ☐ large quantity of beans, buttons, or other counters

Subtraction Designs

Teaching Tips and Extensions

- Have students lay cubes flat on the table or build 3-D designs.
- Provide graph paper instead of the Graph Paper reproducible (page 119).

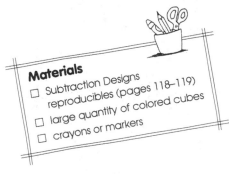

Materials
- ☐ Subtraction Designs reproducibles (pages 118–119)
- ☐ large quantity of colored cubes
- ☐ crayons or markers

A Dollar to Spend

Teaching Tips and Extensions

- ☆ Fill in the prices on the A Dollar to Spend reproducible on page 121. Then, photocopy, cut apart, and laminate the cards.
- Collect small items for students to "purchase." Label each item with a price less than $1.00.
- Show students how to make exchanges with the bank (e.g., a nickel and 5 pennies can be exchanged for 1 dime).

Materials
- ☐ A Dollar to Spend reproducibles (pages 120–121)
- ☐ coins
- ☐ divided container to use for the bank
- ☐ crayons or markers

Subtraction Sock

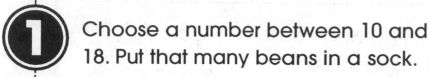

1 Choose a number between 10 and 18. Put that many beans in a sock.

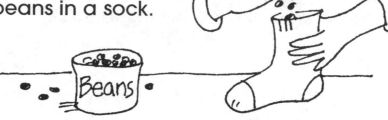

2 Without looking inside, take out some of the beans. Write a subtraction sentence about the beans in the sock and those you took out.

3 Then empty out the sock and check your number sentence.

4 Put all the beans back in the sock and repeat the activity 8 more times. Do the same activity with a different number of beans.

Math Journal Explain your strategy for figuring out how many beans were left in the sock on your journal page.

Instant Math Centers • 2–3 © 2000 Creative Teaching Press

Name _____

Math Journal

Explain your strategy for figuring out
how many beans were left in the sock.

_____

_____

_____

_____

_____

_____

_____

_____

_____

_____

_____

_____

_____

_____

_____

Instant Math Centers • 2–3 © 2000 Creative Teaching Press

Subtraction

Dice Subtraction

 1 Roll 3 dice.

 Match the correct number of counters to each die.

3 Roll 1 die and subtract that number of counters from the total in step 2. Write the subtraction problem on your Dice Subtraction sheet.

4 Repeat the activity 13 more times.

Instant Math Centers • 2–3 © 2000 Creative Teaching Press

Challenge Start with 50 counters. Roll 3 dice and subtract the total from 50 until you reach 0. Write each step as a subtraction problem on the back of your sheet.

Dice Subtraction

Instant Math Centers • 2–3 © 2000 Creative Teaching Press

Subtraction

Subtraction Designs

1 Build a design with 10–18 cubes.
Use 2 different colors.

2 Color your design on your Graph Paper sheet
and write a subtraction sentence to match.

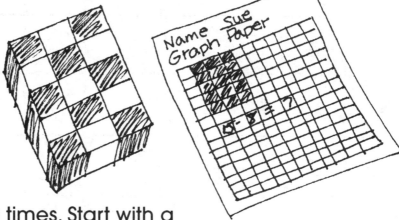

3 Repeat the activity 3 times. Start with a
different number of cubes each time.

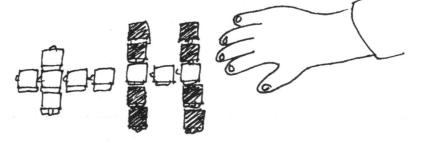

Challenge Pick a number from 10–18. How many different
subtraction fact designs can you build for that number?
Write them on the back of your sheet.

Instant Math Centers • 2–3 © 2000 Creative Teaching Press

Name _____

Graph Paper

Instant Math Centers • 2-3 © 2000 Creative Teaching Press

Subtraction

A Dollar to Spend

1 Pretend you have $1.00 to spend. Count out $1.00 in coins from the bank.

2 Select an item to "buy."

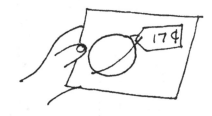

3 Pay for the item with your coins. Write the subtraction problem on a sheet of paper.

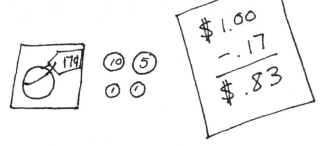

4 Select and pay for more items. Keep going until you have spent the dollar.

Think of 10 things you would like to buy if you had $100.00 to spend. Draw the items on a sheet of paper and label them with prices.

Instant Math Centers • 2–3 © 2000 Creative Teaching Press

A Dollar to Spend

Instant Math Centers • 2-3 © 2000 Creative Teaching Press

Subtraction

Time

These center activities help students develop an awareness of time as they focus on the sequence of events and duration of time. Students should use both digital and standard clocks to practice telling time by the hour, half-hour, quarter-hour, and, if appropriate, by 5-minute intervals.

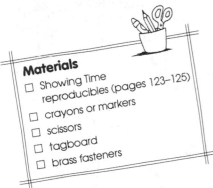

Materials
- ☐ Showing Time reproducibles (pages 123–125)
- ☐ crayons or markers
- ☐ scissors
- ☐ tagboard
- ☐ brass fasteners

Showing Time
Teaching Tips and Extensions

☆ Photocopy the Clock reproducible on tagboard. Students may need adult help inserting the brass fastener through the clock hands and face.

☆ Fill in the times before photocopying the Telling Time Cards reproducible. Vary the times according to the needs of your students.

● The assembled clocks can then be used for the next activity, 30 Minutes Later.

30 Minutes Later
Teaching Tips and Extensions

☆ This activity is to be done following the Showing Time activity, so that the assembled clocks can be used.

● Have students set the clock 15 minutes or 5 minutes earlier or later.

● To challenge older students, start this activity with a time such as 2:10 or 8:35.

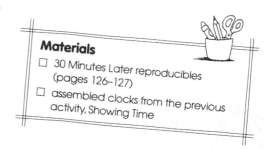

Materials
- ☐ 30 Minutes Later reproducibles (pages 126–127)
- ☐ assembled clocks from the previous activity, Showing Time

Materials
- ☐ Keeping Track of Your Day reproducible (page 128)
- ☐ large stack of plain index cards or similar-sized paper
- ☐ crayons or markers
- ☐ tape
- ☐ several 36" (92 cm) strips of yarn

Keeping Track of Your Day
Teaching Tips and Extensions

● Tell students if you want them to use times on the hour, half-hour, quarter-hour, or 5-minute intervals.

● Before students tape the cards on the yarn, have them shuffle the cards, exchange the cards with a partner, and put their partner's cards in order.

Showing Time

1 Color and cut out the clock face and hands.

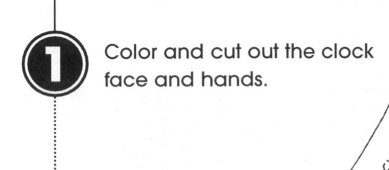

2 Use a brass fastener to put the clock together.

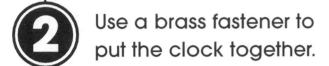

3 Play with a partner. Pick a time card and say the time out loud.

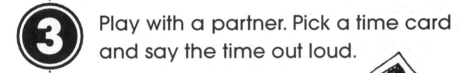

It's 10:15

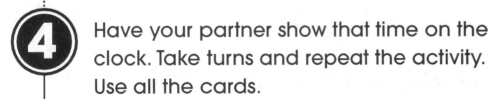

4 Have your partner show that time on the clock. Take turns and repeat the activity. Use all the cards.

Challenge For each card, show the time on the clock 15 minutes later.

Instant Math Centers • 2-3 © 2000 Creative Teaching Press

Time

Clock

Color the parts, cut them out, and attach the hands with a brass fastener.

Instant Math Centers • 2–3 © 2000 Creative Teaching Press

Instant Math Centers • 2–3 © 2000 Creative Teaching Press

Time

30 Minutes Later

1 Play with a partner. Set a clock to the hour or half-hour. Say the time. Write the time on a piece of paper.

2 Have your partner set the clock 30 minutes later, say the time, and write it on your paper.

3 Take turns and repeat the activity 8 more times. Write each time.

Math Journal

Describe what steps you took to set the clock 30 minutes later on your journal page. What would you do to set the clock 1 hour later? 15 minutes later?

Instant Math Centers • 2–3 © 2000 Creative Teaching Press

Math Journal

Describe what steps you took to set the clock 30 minutes later. What would you do to set the clock 1 hour later? 15 minutes later?

I have soccer practice at 4:00. That's 30 minutes from now.

_____

_____

_____

_____

_____

_____

_____

_____

_____

_____

_____

_____

_____

_____

Instant Math Centers • 2–3 © 2000 Creative Teaching Press

Time

Keeping Track of Your Day

1 Use 8 index cards. Draw a picture on each card to show something you do during the day or during the night.

2 Write the time you do each activity on the front of the card. Write your name on the card that shows your first activity of the day.

3 Tape your pictures onto a piece of yarn in the order they happen to create a time line.

Challenge Figure out the amount of time between each activity. Write how much time is between each activity in minutes/hours on a piece of paper.

Instant Math Centers • 2–3 © 2000 Creative Teaching Press